Lori Rowan
9178465333

Lori Rowan
9178465333

Lent: The Road to Redemption, Cycle A

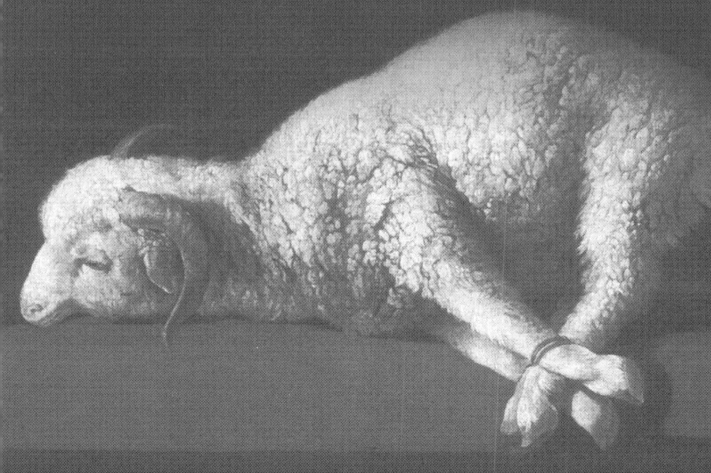

BY LEON SUPRENANT

Published by:
Saint Benedict Press, LLC
PO Box 410487
Charlotte, NC 28241
www.SaintBenedictPress.com

ISBN: 978-1-5051-1704-2

Printed and bound in the United States of America
2020

Lent Cycle A

Table of Contents

Lent Cycle A

Week 1: Temptation in the Desert

Introduction

Lent is our season of repentance and this first Sunday begins the season properly by reminding us that we live in a state of sin. But it also reminds us that there is a way out. The sin that came upon us through Adam can be taken away by the New Adam, Jesus, if we listen to his call to repentance.

For that reason, we'll hear the story of how sin came into the world through Adam and Eve. We'll hear St. Paul explain how that sin was passed down to all their descendants—in other words every human being. Christ undoes what Adam did, obeying instead of disobeying, giving us the escape route the whole world has been looking for.

Finally, we hear the story of Christ's own temptation in the wilderness. He demonstrates the obedience Paul talked about the responses Adam and Eve ought to have given when they were tempted in Eden.

The consciousness of our sin weighs heavy on us during Lent. The Psalm we sing today has long been a favorite response of sinners who know they have sinned. Psalm 51 was written by David after Nathan had confronted him with his own sin: a pretty bad sin at that, since David had arranged for a man to be killed so he could have the man's wife. We call this Psalm the Miserere, after its first word in Latin (*Miserere*, "Have mercy"). Be sure to notice as you are singing the Psalm how perfectly it fits the theme of today's first reading.

Old Testament Reading: Genesis 2:7-9; 3:1-7

Then the Lord God formed man of dust from the ground, and breathed into his nostrils the breath of life; and man became a living being. And the Lord God planted a garden in Eden, in the east; and there he put the man whom he had formed. And out of the ground the Lord God made to grow every tree that is pleasant to the sight and good for food, the tree of life also in the midst of the garden, and the tree of the knowledge of good and evil. Now the serpent was more subtle than any other wild creature that the Lord God had made. He said to the woman, "Did God say, 'You shall not eat of any tree of the garden'?" And the woman said to the serpent, "We may eat of the fruit of the trees of the garden; but God said, 'You shall not eat of the fruit of the tree which is in the midst of the garden, neither shall you touch it, lest you die.'" But the serpent said to the woman, "You will not die. For God knows that when you eat of it your eyes will be opened, and you will be like God, knowing good and evil." So when the woman saw that the tree was good for food, and that it was a delight to the eyes, and that the tree was to be desired to make one wise, she took of its fruit and ate; and she also gave some to her husband, and he ate. Then the eyes of both were opened, and they knew that they were naked; and they sewed fig leaves together and made themselves aprons.

New Testament Reading: Romans 5:12-19

Therefore as sin came into the world through one man and death through sin, and so death spread to all men because all men sinned—sin indeed was in the world before the law was given, but sin is not counted where there is no law. Yet death reigned from Adam to Moses, even over those whose sins were not like the transgression of Adam, who was a type of the one who was to come. But the free gift is not like the trespass. For if many died through one man's trespass, much more have the grace of God and the free gift in the grace of that one man Jesus Christ abounded for many. And the free gift is not like the effect of that one man's sin. For the judgment following one trespass brought condemnation, but the free gift following many trespasses brings justification. If, because of one man's trespass, death reigned through that one man, much more will those who receive the abundance of grace and the free gift of righteousness reign in life through the one man Jesus Christ. Then as one man's trespass led to condemnation for all men, so one man's act of righteousness leads to acquittal and life for all men. For as by one man's disobedience many were made sinners, so by one man's obedience many will be made righteous.

Gospel Reading: Matthew 4:1-11

Then Jesus was led up by the Spirit into the wilderness to be tempted by the devil. And he fasted forty days and forty nights, and afterward he was hungry. And the tempter came and said to him, "If you are the Son of God, command these stones to become loaves of bread." But he answered, "It is written, 'Man shall not live by bread alone, but by every word that proceeds from the mouth of God.'" Then the devil took him to the holy city, and set him on the pinnacle of the temple, and said to him, "If you are the Son of God, throw yourself down; for it is written, 'He will give his angels charge of you,' and 'On their hands they will bear you up, lest you strike your foot against a stone.'" Jesus said to him, "Again it is written, 'You shall not tempt the Lord your God.'" Again, the devil took him to a very high mountain, and showed him all the kingdoms of the world and the glory of them; and he said to him, "All these I will give you, if you will fall down and worship me." Then Jesus said to him, "Begone, Satan! for it is written, 'You shall worship the Lord your God and him only shall you serve.'" Then the devil left him, and behold, angels came and ministered to him.

Points to Ponder

Genesis 2:7-9; 3:1-7

Our first reading comes from Genesis, the first book of the Bible. The name "Genesis" is the Greek word for "beginning," and Genesis tells the story of the beginnings of everything we read about in the rest of the Bible; the world, the human race, the nations of the world, and in particular the nation of Israel. This passage also tells us the story of one of the most puzzling beginnings of all, the beginning of sin.

We all ask questions. Why is there evil in the world and why does God permit it? Is it God's fault? What can we do about it? Genesis answers them with the story of the first man and the first woman. The first part of our story sets the scene. God created man and created a beautiful garden full of every delightful thing for him to live in.

The reading for Mass must be a reasonable length so we will examine additional verses so that we don't miss some of the context. In the Genesis story, after creating the man, Adam (a word that came to mean "man" in Hebrew) and creating the Garden of Eden, God puts the man in the garden giving him one simple instruction:

"The Lord God took the man and put him in the Garden of Eden to till it and keep it. And the Lord God commanded the man, saying, "You may freely eat of every tree of the garden; but of the tree of the knowledge of good and evil you shall not eat, for in the day that you eat of it you shall die."

Immediately after that, God declared, "It is not good that the man should be alone; I will make him a helper fit for him.". God created all the animals, but one by one Adam discovers that none of them will do for a helper.

"So the Lord God caused a deep sleep to fall upon the man, and while he slept took one of his ribs and closed up its place with flesh; and the rib which the Lord God had taken from the man he made into a woman and brought her to the man. Then the man said, "This at last is bone of my bones and flesh of my flesh; she shall be called Woman, because she was taken out of Man." Therefore a man leaves his father and his mother and cleaves to his wife, and they become one flesh. And the man and his wife were both naked, and were not ashamed."

In this section of Genesis we see the beginning of marriage, a partnership of two of the same kind of creature. No beast was a suitable "helper" for Adam. God had to create woman from the same stuff as man, so that he would recognize her as another of the same kind. And they "were both naked, and were not ashamed," because shame comes in only where there is something to be ashamed of. There was no sin in the Garden of Eden—not yet.

The second part of our reading deals with the temptation by the serpent, Satan!

How do we know the serpent is Satan? Most of us probably don't even ask that question—we've associated the serpent with Satan since the first time we heard this story. In fact Genesis doesn't tell us explicitly who the serpent was. The serpent's identity is revealed at the other end of the Bible—in the Book of Revelation, where he is called "that ancient serpent, who is called the Devil and Satan, the deceiver of the whole world" (Revelation 12:1).

Satan argues with Eve first. She is reluctant: she remembers what God said about the fruit, and it takes some fast-talking from Satan to overcome her reluctance. She then hands some of the fruit to Adam and he compliantly takes and eats it. "*Then the eyes of both were opened, and they knew that they were naked.*" Now they know the difference between good and evil because they know they have done evil and they were ashamed of being seen by God. The only reason shame occurs to them is because they have fallen.

They have sinned: they have broken God's commandment, and (as we know) he will drive them out of paradise. But worse than losing paradise is losing the relationship of perfect trust and love they once had with God. How can what they have broken ever be repaired? This is the central problem in the history of humanity. And the rest of today's readings will tell us the solution.

Do we take this story in Genesis literally? The Catholic Church actually has no official position on that. The Catechism tells us that the writers of Genesis used "figurative language" (CCC 390) in writing about the Fall but they were writing about a thing that really happened: our ancestors' fall from grace. Scripture tells us the moral and theological truth of our humanity: that we were created in the image of God, that we were created good, and that we fell from grace through our own sin. To be Catholic, we must believe these things—but we have the freedom to investigate human beginnings as much as we like within those assumptions. Many Catholics accept scientific theories of human evolution, and interpret Genesis figuratively. Others believe that the accounts in Genesis are literally true history. Both can be good Catholic Christians. The important thing is to understand the moral and theological truth, and that is the only thing the Church insists on.

Romans 5:12-19

St. Paul tells us, the answer to the problem of sin, is the obedience of Jesus Christ. Adam, Paul says, "was a type of the one who was to come." The word "type" comes from a Greek word meaning "image" or "model," like the image left when you press a seal into clay or wax or when you press an inked letter into a page. When we talk about a "type" in Scripture, we usually mean something in the Old Testament that is an image or model for something in the New Testament. Theologians use the word *typology* to describe the study of these "types."

For example, we say that Noah's Flood is a "type" of our baptism. Like the waters of the Flood, baptism washes away sin, leaving us a purified new creation. In the same way, we say that the Exodus from Egypt is a "type" of our redemption through Christ. Israel was freed from bondage to the power of Egypt, and we are freed from bondage to the power of sin. The Old Testament event foreshadows a greater fulfillment in the New Testament.

In Paul's comparison of Adam and Jesus, the image is something like a mirror image. Christ undoes what Adam did. Adam sinned and disobeyed the Lord; Jesus Christ obeyed even to death on the cross. Adam's sin brings death; Christ's obedience brings life.

"How is he a type?" someone will ask. Why, in that, as Adam became to those who were sprung from him—although they had not eaten of the tree—the cause of that death which by his eating was introduced, so too did Christ become to those sprung from Him, even though they had not wrought righteousness, the Provider of that righteousness which through his cross he graciously bestowed on us all.

—*St. John Chrysostom, Homily 10 on Romans*

We are all born tainted by sin because of our first parents' transgression: that's what we mean when we talk about the doctrine of *original sin*. By sending his Son to undo that damage, God redeems us from sin. It doesn't happen because we were very good and finally deserved life instead of death; it happens because God chooses to give us a gift—freely, out of his own overflowing love. When we are baptized, the long chain of sin that ties us to Adam and Eve is broken, as St. Augustine explains:

"By the water that holds forth the sacrament of grace in its outward form, and by the Spirit who bestows the benefit of grace in its inward power, canceling the bond of guilt, and restoring the goodness of nature, the man, who derived his first birth originally from Adam alone, is regenerated in Christ alone."

—*St. Augustine, Letter 98, 2*

We are given a chance to be born all over again in Christ and because of that gift, we are no longer slaves to sin and death. St. Aphrahat has a colorful and dramatic interpretation of St. Paul's phrase, "death reigned from Adam to Moses." He imagines a personified Death trembling before the declaration, "I am the God of Abraham, the God of Isaac, and the God of Jacob."

"And why did he say, "death reigned from Adam to Moses"? Who is so ignorant as to imagine that only from Adam to Moses has death reigned?

Yet we should understand from what he said here: "death spread to all men." Thus, death spread to all from Moses until the world ends.

Yet Moses preached that its kingdom is made void.

For when Adam broke the commandment by which the sentence of death was passed upon his progeny, Death hoped that he would bind fast all the sons of man and would be king over them for ever. But when Moses came, he proclaimed the resurrection, and Death knew that his kingdom is to be made void.

For Moses said, "Let Reuben live, and not die, nor let his men be few" [Deuteronomy 33:6]. And when the Holy One called Moses from the bush, he said this to him: "I am the God of Abraham, the God of Isaac, and the God of Jacob" [Exodus 3:6].

When Death heard this utterance, he trembled and feared and was terrified and was greatly disturbed, and knew that he had not become king forever over the children of Adam. From the hour that he heard God saying to Moses, "I am the God of Abraham, the God of Isaac, and the God of Jacob," Death wrung his hands, for he learned that God is King of the dead and of the living, and that it is appointed to the children of Adam to come forth from his darkness and rise with their bodies.

And observe that our Redeemer Jesus also, when he repeated this saying to the Sadducees, when they were arguing with him about the resurrection of the dead, said this: "Now he is not God of the dead, but of the living; for all live to him" [Luke 20:38]."

—*St. Aphrahat, Demonstration 22, 2*

This is very much in keeping with St. Paul's typological interpretation of the Old Testament. The Fathers of the Church, like the apostles and Jesus himself, saw the events and sayings in the Old Testament as foreshadows of the great things that were to come in the age of the Messiah.

Matthew 4:1-11

Jesus goes through the same temptation that our first parents went through. Notice how the devil's technique hasn't changed in all those thousands of years. He still deals in half-truths and lofty promises of God-like power. He's even still using food as a temptation.

That's the devil's first try, temptation number one out of three. Jesus has been out in the desert for a long time. He's a human being: he has to be hungry but he can fix that, can't he? He's the Son of God. He has all the power in the world. God spoke the universe into being; it shouldn't be hard to command a few stones to turn into bread.

Hunger and loneliness are powerful things, and St. John Chrysostom was convinced that the devil was especially apt to make use of them.

You shall not put the Lord, your God, to the test.

"And look where the Spirit led him when he had taken him: not into a city and forum, but into a wilderness. That is, because he wanted to attract the devil, he gives him a handle not only by his hunger, but also by the place. For the devil attacks people most especially when he sees them left alone and by themselves. In just the same way he set upon the woman in the beginning, having caught her alone, and found her apart from her husband—just as when he sees us with others and banded together, he is not equally confident, and makes no attack. Thus we have the greatest need for this very reason to be flocking together continually, so that we may not be open to the devil's attacks."

—*St. John Chrysostom*
Homily 13 on Matthew

Jesus refuses to give in to temptation. There are things more important than his hunger: "Man shall not live by bread alone, but by every word that proceeds from the mouth of God." He will not be tempted away from obedience to his Father by the grumbling in his stomach. As St. Irenaeus points out, it is here that Jesus is in effect reversing the Fall by giving the answer Adam and Eve ought to have given: "Thus the corruption of man, which happened in paradise by both Adam and Eve eating, was done away with by his lack of food in this world." (Irenaeus, *Against Heresies*, 5.21.2.)

The second temptation asks Jesus to prove that he really is the Son of God. The devil takes him to "the pinnacle of the temple," which was certainly the tallest man-made thing in Jerusalem at the time. Depending on exactly what Matthew means by the "pinnacle," Jesus could easily have been at the height of a small skyscraper.

Why shouldn't he just throw himself off? Wouldn't that be a spectacular way to prove he was the Son of God? Everyone would believe he was the Messiah if they actually saw the angels bearing him up.

"Why is it that at each temptation he adds this, "If you are the Son of God?" He is doing much the same thing he did in the former case. That is, just as he then slandered God, saying, "when you eat of it your eyes will be opened," thereby intending to signify, that they were beguiled and over-reached, and had received no benefit; even so in this case also he insinuates this same thing, saying, "In vain God has called you Son, and has beguiled you with his gift. If that isn't true, give us some clear proof that you have that power." Then, because Christ had reasoned with him from Scripture, he also brings in a testimony of the prophet."
—*St. John Chrysostom Homily 13 on Matthew*

Again Christ refuses. So the devil tries one last time. Showing him all the kingdoms of the earth, the devil offers them all to him, on one condition: Christ must fall down and worship him. Power is as tempting as food—even more so, perhaps, because power is very tempting to good people. Think of all the good you could do if you were made dictator of the earth! Doubtless every dictator has thought the same thing. Think of all the good I could do if only I had power—and then, think of all the good I could still accomplish if only I stayed in power.

Christ knows that earthly power is not what he is here for. In fact, he can only accomplish his mission by becoming utterly powerless. So he dismisses the devil, and then—only after all the temptations are over—angels come to serve him.

Lenten Moment

Resisting temptation

Catholics have a tradition of giving up something for Lent. In addition to the fasts prescribed by our tradition, people will often pick one particular thing they like and give it up as a sign of repentance. Some people give up chocolate; others might give up television. It's a way of reminding ourselves that "Man shall not live by bread alone, but by every word that proceeds from the mouth of God." But are we giving up what really tempts us? Think about it. If you're really, really into television, did you decide to give up chocolate? If you really, really care whether people think you look good, did you decide to give up fattening foods? The devil is very clever with his temptations. He even quotes Scripture to tempt Christ. He can easily convince us to give in to the things that really tempt us while giving up a few things we don't really care about nearly as much.

So how do we resist temptation like that? St. Augustine suggests that we should look at the temptation of Christ, not just for general inspiration but also to imitate Christ's example of resisting temptation.

Learn from the temptation of Christ. If we listen to his answers to the devil, so that we may answer the same way when we ourselves are tempted, we are then *entering through the gate*, as you have heard it read in the Gospel. What does it mean to enter by the gate? To enter by Christ, who himself said, "I am the door" (John 10:7). And to enter through Christ is to imitate his ways.

—*Augustine, Exposition on Psalm 91*

Catechism Connections

- To understand more about how important it is to acknowledge the fact of sin, see CCC 386-387.

- To find out more about how the Church understands the story of the Fall in Genesis, see CCC 389.

- To understand the nature of Adam and Eve's sin, see CCC 397-398.

- To learn more about the consequences of Adam and Eve's sin, see CCC 402-406.

- To understand Christ's obedience better, see CCC 606-612.

- To learn more about how baptism washes away sin, see CCC 977-980.

Rome to Home

The Council of Trent solemnly expressed the Church's faith concerning original sin. In the previous catechesis we considered that Council's teaching in regard to the personal sin of our first parents. Now we wish to reflect on what the Council said about the consequences of that sin for humanity.

In this regard the Tridentine decree states first of all:

Adam's sin has passed to all his descendants, that is, to all men and women as descendants of our first parents, and their heirs, in human nature already deprived of God's friendship.

The Tridentine decree (cf. DS 1512) explicitly states that Adam's sin tainted not only himself but also all his descendants. Adam forfeited original justice and holiness not only for himself, but also "for us" (*nobis etiam*).

Therefore he transmitted to the whole human race not only bodily death and other penalties (consequences of sin), but also sin itself as the death of the soul (*peccatum quod mors est animae*). ...

The Tridentine decree contains another statement: Adam's sin is transmitted to all his descendants by generation and not merely by way of bad example. The decree states: "This sin of Adam, which by origin is unique and transmitted by generation and not by way of imitation, is present in all as proper to each" (DS 1513).

Therefore original sin is transmitted by way of natural generation. This conviction of the Church is indicated also by the practice of infant baptism, to which the conciliar decree refers. Newborn infants are incapable of committing personal sin, yet in accordance with the Church's centuries-old tradition, they are baptized shortly after birth for the remission of sin. The decree states: "They are truly baptized for the remission of sin, so that what they contracted in generation may be cleansed by regeneration" (DS 1514).

In this context it is evident that original sin in Adam's descendants does not have the character of personal guilt. It is the privation of sanctifying grace in a nature which has been diverted from its supernatural end through the fault of the first parents. It is a "sin of nature," only analogically comparable to "personal sin." In the state of original justice, before sin, sanctifying grace was like a supernatural "endowment" of human nature. The loss of grace is contained in the inner "logic" of sin, which is a rejection of the will of God, who bestows this gift. Sanctifying grace has ceased to constitute the supernatural enrichment of that nature which the first parents passed on to all their descendants in the state in which it existed when human generation began. Therefore man is conceived and born without sanctifying grace. It is precisely this "initial state" of man, linked to his origin, that constitutes the essence of original sin as a legacy (peccatum originale originatum, as it is usually called).

—*Pope John Paul II, General Audience, October 1, 1986.*

Voices of the Saints

"Do not let temptations frighten you; they are the trials of the soul whom God wants to test when He knows that he is strong enough to sustain the battle and weave his garland of glory with his own hands."

—*St. Padre Pio*

Study Questions

1. What material did God use to make man and how did the man become a living being? (See Genesis 2:7-9 & Points to Ponder)

2. When did the man and the woman begin to feel ashamed of being naked? (See Genesis 3:7)

3. According to St. Paul, of whom is Adam an image or model? What difference does obedience of Christ make to the disobedience of Adam? (See Points to Ponder)

4. What did man do to deserve justification through Christ? (See Points to Ponder)

5. What was the first temptation the devil tried against Christ? Why is this particular temptation significant and what is the connection to events in the Garden of Eden? (See Matthew 4: 2-3 and Points to Ponder)

6. In Matthew's account, what was the second temptation?

7. Again in Matthew's account, what was the third temptation?

Notes

Lent Cycle A

Week 2: Transfiguration

Introduction

What seems like a miscellaneous group of readings turns out to have one common thread: placing the coming of Christ firmly in the long story that we call "salvation history."

First, we read of God calling Abraham, the event that marks the beginning of the Israelite nation. St. Paul will then tell us that we are called in a similar way, and that the grace we have through Jesus Christ did not come to us when Christ appeared on earth in Paul's lifetime, but "ages ago." Finally, the Gospel shows us Jesus in glory talking with Moses and Elijah, who together represent the entire Old Testament. Combined these three readings displays the unity of Scripture: though they are made up of dozens of different books written over the course of thousands of years by very different authors, together they form one story of our salvation from beginning to end.

Old Testament Reading: Genesis 12:1-4

Now the LORD said to Abram, "Go from your country and your kindred and your father's house to the land that I will show you. And I will make of you a great nation, and I will bless you, and make your name great, so that you will be a blessing. I will bless those who bless you, and him who curses you I will curse; and by you all the families of the earth shall bless themselves." So Abram went, as the LORD had told him; and Lot went with him. Abram was seventy-five years old when he departed from Haran.

New Testament Reading: 2 Timothy 1:8-10

Do not be ashamed then of testifying to our Lord, nor of me his prisoner, but share in suffering for the gospel in the power of God, who saved us and called us with a holy calling, not in virtue of our works but in virtue of his own purpose and the grace which he gave us in Christ Jesus ages ago, and now has manifested through the appearing of our Savior Christ Jesus, who abolished death and brought life and immortality to light through the gospel.

Our strength comes from God even if it will not be easy. (handwritten)

God makes an unconditional promise (handwritten, left margin)

Gospel Reading: Matthew 17:1-9

And after six days Jesus took with him Peter and James and John his brother, and led them up a high mountain apart. And he was transfigured before them, and his face shone like the sun, and his garments became white as light. And behold, there appeared to them Moses and Elijah, talking with him. And Peter said to Jesus, "Lord, it is well that we are here; if you wish, I will make three booths here, one for you and one for Moses and one for Elijah." He was still speaking, when lo, a bright cloud overshadowed them, and a voice from the cloud said, "This is my beloved Son, with whom I am well pleased; listen to him." When the disciples heard this, they fell on their faces, and were filled with awe. But Jesus came and touched them, saying, "Rise, and have no fear." And when they lifted up their eyes, they saw no one but Jesus only. And as they were coming down the mountain, Jesus commanded them, "Tell no one the vision, until the Son of man is raised from the dead."

Points to Ponder

Genesis 12:1-4

Genesis is the book of beginnings, and here is one of the most important beginnings in Scripture: the beginning of the nation of Israel. This is important because the Israelites are God's chosen people: "Salvation is from the Jews," Jesus will tell us next week. The entire Old Testament after Genesis will tell the story of Israel's successes and—more often—failures, all of it pointing to and looking forward to the coming of the Messiah.

In this short reading, God calls Abram (who will later be called Abraham) from a comfortable life in Haran, leaving everything he knew—"Go from your country and your kindred and your father's house"—to take up a wandering life with an uncertain destination. Notice that Abram is already 75 years old. He's not an ambitious young man with his whole life ahead of him and all the time in the world to make mistakes. He's already an old man, with his youth behind him, and setting out on an unknown adventure is a pretty big deal. All he knows is that God has promised to make a great nation out of him, and to show him a land that will belong to him eventually. He doesn't know where this land will be, and the great nation promised will occur after he's dead.

Nevertheless, Abram doesn't ask questions. He does what God asks him to do. This example of faith was a great favorite among the earliest Christians. As the Letter to the Hebrews 11:8 reminds its readers: "By faith Abraham obeyed when he was called to go out to a place which he was to receive as an inheritance; and he went out, not knowing where he was to go."

St. Paul also points out in Romans that Abraham lived before the Law, and yet Abraham is the model of faith and righteousness. Therefore, righteousness comes, not from the Law, but from faith in God. All who believe are descendants of Abraham—not just the Israelites but also every other Christian believer.

The promise to Abraham and his descendants, that they should inherit the world, did not come through the law but through the righteousness of faith. If it is the adherents of the law who are to be the heirs, faith is null and the promise is void. For the law brings wrath, but where there is no law there is no transgression. That is why it depends on faith, in order that the promise may rest

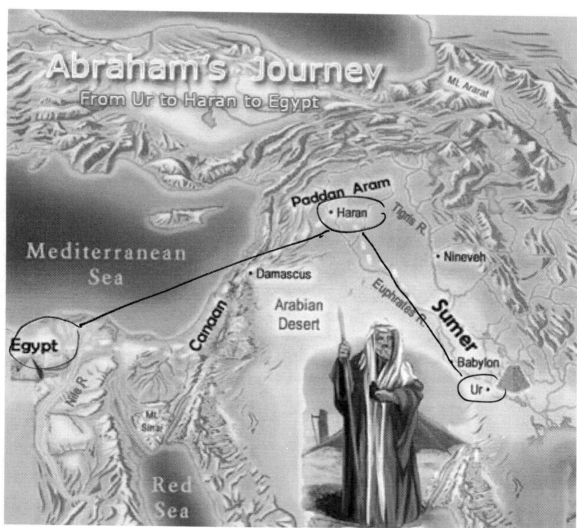

Abraham's Journey — From Ur to Haran to Egypt

Handwritten notes:
Abram = Abraham
his son is Isaac
He had at 100 and he died at 140

Before 10 Commandments

all 3 religious believe in Abraham

Muslim Jew + christian

on grace and be guaranteed to all his descendants—not only to the adherents of the law but also to those who share the faith of Abraham, for he is the father of us all, as it is written, "I have made you the father of many nations"—in the presence of the God in whom he believed, who gives life to the dead and calls into existence the things that do not exist.

Romans 4:13-17

This calling of Abram is one of the most important events in history, because it's the beginning of the Israelite nation. But it's also important to each of us personally, because it's the pattern for our own calling—as we'll see in the New Testament reading.

2 Timothy 1:8-10

In this letter, we're reminded that God called us as he called Abram, and like Abram, we have to face uncertainty and suffering on our way to the land of promise.

But we can't let uncertainty deter us because we have the certainty of the Gospel.

It's easy for us to take that certainty for granted in comfortable times. Let's think for a moment what things were like when this second letter to Timothy was written.

When Paul says, "Do not be ashamed then of testifying to our Lord," we have to remember that there were very good reasons for people to be ashamed. Jesus Christ had died the disgraceful death assigned to the worst criminals. Crucifixion wasn't just execution and it wasn't just torture: it was specifically designed as a public display of disgrace. The family and friends of a crucified criminal would hardly dare show their faces in public. Its as though Paul is telling Timothy, "Do not be ashamed to It was as acknowledge that you are suffering persecution for a Lord, who was executed as though he were a terrorist leader." Then there's Paul himself, "his prisoner"—again, not a thing that looks good on a resume. This is when we rely on the grace of our faith. We know that the disgrace of the crucifixion led to the glory of the resurrection. We know that all the trials we endure now are leading us to resurrected glory with Christ.

Like Abram, we are called "with a holy calling, not in virtue of our works but in virtue of his own purpose and the grace that he gave us in Christ Jesus ages ago." When these words were written, Christ's ministry was a living memory. It was not "ages ago," any more than the papacy of John Paul II is "ages ago" to us. Clearly what Paul means is that we were called because it was always God's plan to call us. We live in time, but God's plan for us is eternal.

Matthew 17:1-9

The Transfiguration is a strange episode in the Gospel; a moment when divine glory suddenly breaks through into the ordinary human lives of three of Jesus' disciples. It clearly overwhelms them; Peter's response looks like babbling, as if he is desperately trying to think of some appropriate way to respond to a situation that simply has no precedent. In fact, in Mark's account of the Transfiguration, he explicitly adds, "For he did not know what to say, for they were exceedingly afraid" (Mark 9:6). He suggests putting up three tents, as Jews did during the Feast of Booths—perhaps not the most practical response, though it's hard to imagine what would be a practical response. Overwhelmed or not, Peter, James, and John recognize that this is an encounter with the divine. The familiar signs from the Old Testament are there.

Jesus led the three disciples up a high mountain:

The LORD said to Moses, "Come up to me on the mountain, and wait there..."

Exodus 24:12

Jesus' face shone like the sun:

When Moses came down from Mount Sinai, carrying the two tablets of the testimony, he did not realize that the skin of his face shone because he had been talking with God..

Exodus 34: 29

A bright cloud overshadowed them on the mountain:

The glory of the LORD settled on Mount Sinai, and the cloud covered it six days.

Exodus 24:16

A voice came from the cloud:

"And the LORD said to Moses, "Lo, I am coming to you in a thick cloud, that the people may hear when I speak with you, and may also believe you for ever." —*Exodus 19:9*

Why did Christ reveal his divine glory to his three closest friends at this particular moment? St. Leo the Great tells us that it was partly to keep them from fear and despair when they realized that he was going to suffer and die. St. Leo the Great was a pope who knew something about fear and despair: he faced down Attila the Hun who was poised to destroy Rome with his invincible horde and somehow persuaded him to turn back. St. Leo believed that the main purpose of the Transfiguration was to keep the disciples from fear and despair when Jesus was crucified. Indeed, if you read the verses that follow right after today's Gospel reading Jesus foretold his own suffering. We should also keep in mind that this passage is a preview of our own transfiguration: it shows Christ's disciples what they will eventually become in the resurrection.

"And in this Transfiguration the foremost object was to remove the scandal of the cross from the disciples' hearts, and to prevent their faith being disturbed by the humiliation of his voluntary suffering by revealing to them the excellence of his hidden dignity. But with no less foresight, the foundation was laid of the Holy Church's hope, that the whole body of Christ might realize the character of the change which it would have to receive, and that the members might promise themselves a share in that honor which had already shone forth in their Head. About which the Lord had himself said, when he spoke of the majesty of his coming, "Then the righteous will shine like the sun in the kingdom of their Father" [Matthew 13:43], while the blessed Apostle Paul bears witness to the very same thing, and says: I consider that the sufferings of this present time are not worth comparing with the that is to be revealed to us" [Romans 8:18]: and again, "For you have died, and your life is hid with Christ in God. When Christ who is our life appears, then you also will appear with him in glory" [Colossians 3:3]."

St. Leo also points out the importance of the appearance of Moses and Elijah. Jewish tradition referred to the whole of the Scriptures (that is, what we call the Old Testament) as "the Law and the Prophets." Law (Moses) and the Prophets.

"Think not that I have come to abolish the law and the prophets; I have come not to abolish them but to fulfil them." —*Matthew 5:17*

"So whatever you wish that men would do to you, do so to them; for this is the law and the prophets. " —*Matthew 7:12*

"You shall love the Lord your God with all your heart, and with all your soul, and with all your mind. This is the great and first commandment. And a second is like it, You shall love your neighbor as yourself. On these two commandments depend all the law and the prophets." —*Matthew 22:37-40.*

After the reading of the law and the prophets, the rulers of the synagogue sent to them, saying, "Brethren, if you have any word of exhortation for the people, say it." —*Acts 13:15*

Moses was the great lawgiver, and the traditional author of the Torah—the books of Genesis, Exodus, Leviticus, Numbers, and Deuteronomy, which were collectively called the Law. Elijah was the greatest of the prophets (after Moses), and the one who was expected to return before the Messiah came—a prediction that Christ tells his disciples (in the verses that immediately follow our Gospel reading) was fulfilled in John the Baptist:

And the disciples asked him, "Then why do the scribes say that first Elijah must come?" He replied, "Elijah does come, and he is to restore all things; but I tell you that Elijah has already come, and they did not know him, but did to him whatever they pleased. So also the Son of man will suffer at their hands."

—*Matthew 17:10-12*

Thus Moses and Elijah stand together representing the whole of the Law and the Prophets, according to St. Leo:

"But to confirm the Apostles and assist them to all knowledge, still further instruction was conveyed by that miracle. For Moses and Elijah—that is, the Law and the Prophets—appeared talking with the Lord; that in the presence of those five men might most truly be fulfilled what was said: In two or three witnesses stands every word [see Deuteronomy 19:15]. Is there anything more stable and reliable than this word, in the proclamation of which the trumpet of the Old and of the New Testament joins, and the documentary evidence of the ancient witnesses combine with the teaching of the Gospel? For the pages of both Testaments corroborate each other. Under the veil of mysteries, the types that went before promised the One who is now displayed clearly and conspicuously by the splendor of the present glory. Because, as says the blessed John, "the law was given through Moses; grace and truth came through Jesus Christ" [John 1:17], in whom is fulfilled both the promise of prophetic figures and the purpose of the laws: for he both teaches the truth of prophecy by his presence, and renders the commands possible through grace."

—*St. Leo the Great, Sermon 51, 3.*

Lenten Moment

The Transfiguration was a real event that happened in history, witnessed by three real people who were overwhelmed by what they saw. Both the Church Father Origen and Pope St. John Paul II tell us that the Transfiguration is something we can experience for ourselves, in our own moment of history.

It involves climbing a mountain—"an image dear to mystics," as Pope John Paul reminds us. What does the image represent? It's a picture of what it's like to "get away from it all."

If you've ever climbed a mountain and stood at the top, you know how far away the world below seems. You can see it clearly, but you're also detached from it. The towns and cities below go about their daily business, but it doesn't seem to concern you anymore the way it does when you're down there in the middle of it.

And that's something like the experience the mystics are inviting us to share. When you detach yourself from your worldly concerns and focus on what's really important—your relationship with God—it's like climbing a mountain and getting away from the bustle of the town below. In the clear silence of your contemplation, you're open to an experience of divinity.

However, you must leave the world behind, and that's why Lent is an ideal time to climb that mountain. Lent encourages us to give up the things we love most in this world—things that are good in themselves, like chocolate or beer, but that can keep our attention in the valley rather than on the mountaintop. With them out of the way, and our attention turned toward heaven, we might be granted a glimpse of the glory that Peter, James, and John saw.

Catechism Connections

- To see how the Church understands the place of the Transfiguration in our faith, see CCC 554-556.

- To understand the context for the voice from the cloud, see CCC 444.

- For more on the symbolism of cloud and light, see CCC 697.

- To understand Elijah's place in the Old Testament, and how he looked forward to Christ, see CCC 2581-2584.

- To understand what contemplative prayer is and how we enter into it, see CCC 2709-2719.

Rome to Home

At Matins for the Transfiguration the Eastern liturgy again sings: "Immutable brightness of the Father's light, O Word, in your shining light on Tabor we have seen today the light that is the Father and the light that is the Spirit, a light that illumines all creation."

This liturgical text emphasizes the Trinitarian dimension of Christ's Transfiguration on the mountain. In fact, the Father's presence with his revealing voice is explicit. Christian tradition catches an implicit glimpse of the Holy Spirit's presence based on the parallel event of the Baptism in the Jordan, when the Spirit descended upon Christ like a dove (cf. Mk 1: 10). Indeed, the Father's command: "Listen to him" (Mk 9: 7) presupposes that Jesus was filled with the Holy Spirit so that his words would be "spirit and life" (Jn 6: 63; cf. 3: 34-35).

It is possible, then, to climb the mountain in order to pause, to contemplate and to be immersed in the mystery of God's light. Tabor represents all the mountains that lead us to God, according to an image dear to mystics. Another text of the Eastern Church invites us to make this ascent to the summit and the light: "Come, peoples, follow me! Let us climb the holy and heavenly mountain; let us spiritually pause in the city of the living God and contemplate in spirit the divinity of the Father and the Holy Spirit which is resplendent in the Only-begotten Son" (troparion at the conclusion of the *Canon of St. John Damascene*).

In the Transfiguration we not only contemplate the mystery of God, passing from light to light (cf. Ps 36: 10), but we are also invited to listen to the divine word that is addressed to us. Above the word of the Law in Moses and of the prophecy in Elijah, the voice of the Father can be heard referring to the voice of the Son, as I have just mentioned. In presenting his "beloved Son," the Father adds the invitation to listen to him (cf. Mk 9: 7).

—*Pope John Paul II, General Audience, April 26, 2000.*

Voices of the Saints

"At his Transfiguration Christ showed his disciples the splendor of his beauty, to which he will shape and color those who are his: 'He will reform our lowness configured to the body of his glory'" (Philippians 3:21)

—*St. Thomas Aquinas, Summa Theologiae*

Study Questions

1. In our Old Testament reading what does Abram know about where God is telling him to go?

2. How is the calling of Abraham similar to the calling of Jesus' disciples? How is it similar to the calling of an ordinary Catholic Christian in an ordinary parish today?

3. What is St. Paul trying to convey in his 2nd letter to Timothy when he says that God gave us grace in Christ Jesus "ages ago"?

4. How did Peter react to the Lord's Transfiguration?

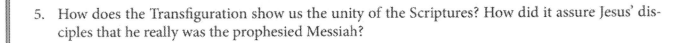

5. How does the Transfiguration show us the unity of the Scriptures? How did it assure Jesus' disciples that he really was the prophesied Messiah?

6. How does the Transfiguration account parallel Moses' encounters with God in the Old Testament?

Lent Cycle A

Week 3: The Messiah

Introduction

Water is our theme for this Sunday: living water that quenches our thirst in the desert.

For a Christian, of course, water immediately brings baptism to mind. And that is the real subject of this collection of readings: not the water that quenches our thirst until we get thirsty again an hour later but the water of eternal life that Christ offers us, no matter who we are or how little the world thinks of us.

We begin with the story of Israel grumbling in the desert because of the lack of water. Today's Psalm asks us to remember the story of Israel in the desert, and pleads with us not to make the same mistake: "O that today you would hearken to his voice! Harden not your hearts, as at Meribah, as on the day at Massah in the wilderness, when your fathers tested me, and put me to the proof, though they had seen my work." (Psalm 95:7-9.)

Old Testament Reading: Exodus 17:3-7

But the people thirsted there for water, and the people murmured against Moses, and said, "Why did you bring us up out of Egypt, to kill us and our children and our cattle with thirst?" So Moses cried to the LORD, "What shall I do with this people? They are almost ready to stone me." And the LORD said to Moses, "Pass on before the people, taking with you some of the elders of Israel; and take in your hand the rod with which you struck the Nile, and go. Behold, I will stand before you there on the rock at Horeb; and you shall strike the rock, and water shall come out of it, that the people may drink." And Moses did so, in the sight of the elders of Israel. And he called the name of the place Massah and Meribah, because of the faultfinding of the children of Israel, and because they put the LORD to the proof by saying, "Is the LORD among us or not?"

replace it w/ a virtue

New Testament Reading: Romans 5:1-2, 5-8

Therefore, since we are justified by faith, we have peace with God through our Lord Jesus Christ. Through him we have obtained access to this grace in which we stand, and we rejoice in our hope of sharing the glory of God. ...And hope does not disappoint us, because God's love has been poured into our hearts through the Holy Spirit which has been given to us. While we were still weak, at the right time Christ died for the ungodly. Why, one will hardly die for a righteous man—though perhaps for a good man one will dare even to die. But God shows his love for us in that while we were yet sinners Christ died for us.

Gospel Reading: John 4:5-42

So he came to a city of Samaria, called Sychar, near the field that Jacob gave to his son Joseph. Jacob's well was there, and so Jesus, wearied as he was with his journey, sat down beside the well. It was about the sixth hour. There came a woman of Samaria to draw water. Jesus said to her, "Give me a drink." For his disciples had gone away into the city to buy food. The Samaritan woman said to him, "How is it that you, a Jew, ask a drink of me, a woman of Samaria?" For Jews have no dealings with Samaritans. Jesus answered her, "If you knew the gift of God, and who it is that is saying to you, 'Give me a drink,' you would have asked him, and he would have given you living water." The woman said to him, "Sir, you have nothing to draw with, and the well is deep; where do you get that living water? Are you greater than our father Jacob, who gave us the well, and drank from it himself, and his sons, and his cattle?" Jesus said to her, "Every one who drinks of this water will thirst again, but whoever drinks of the water that I shall give him will never thirst; the water that I shall give him will become in him a spring of water welling up to eternal life." The woman said to him, "Sir, give me this water, that I may not thirst, nor come here to draw." Jesus said to her, "Go, call your husband, and come here." The woman answered him, "I have no husband." Jesus said to her, "You are right in saying, 'I have no husband'; for you have had five husbands, and he whom you now have is not your husband; this you said truly." The woman said to him, "Sir, I perceive that you are a prophet. Our fathers worshiped on this mountain; and you say that in Jerusalem is the place where men ought to worship." Jesus said to her, "Woman, believe me, the hour is coming when neither on this mountain nor in Jerusalem will you worship the Father. You worship what you do not know; we worship what we know, for salvation is from the Jews. But the hour is coming, and now is, when the true worshipers will worship the Father in spirit and truth, for such the Father seeks to worship him. God is spirit, and those who worship him must worship in spirit and truth." The woman said to him, "I know that Messiah is coming (he who is called Christ); when he comes, he will show us all things." Jesus said to her, "I who speak to you am he." Just then his disciples came. They marveled that he was talking with a woman, but none said, "What do you wish?" or, "Why are you talking with her?" So the woman left her water jar, and went away into the city, and said to the people, "Come, see a man who told me all that I ever did. Can this be the Christ?" They went out of the city and were coming to him. Meanwhile the disciples besought him, saying, "Rabbi, eat." But he said to them, "I have food to eat of which you do not know." So the disciples said to one another, "Has any one brought him food?" Jesus said to them, "My food is to do the will of him who sent me, and to accomplish his work. Do you not say, 'There are yet four months, then comes the harvest'? I tell you, lift up your eyes, and see how the fields are already white for harvest. He who reaps receives wages, and gathers fruit for eternal life, so that sower and reaper may rejoice together. For here the saying holds true, 'One sows and an-other reaps.' I sent you to reap that for which you did not labor; others have labored, and you have entered into their labor." Many Samaritans from that city believed in him because of the woman's testimony, "He told me all that I ever did." So when the Samaritans came to him, they asked him to stay with them; and he stayed there two days. And many more believed because of his word. They said to the woman, "It is no longer because of your words that we believe, for we have heard for ourselves, and we know that this is indeed the Savior of the world."

Points to Ponder

First Reading: Exodus 17:3-7

There are actually two similar but very different stories of Moses striking a rock to get water for the people. Our Old Testament Reading this week is the first one, the second is in the book of Numbers:

Now there was no water for the congregation; and they assembled themselves together against Moses and against Aaron. And the people contended with Moses, and said, "Would that we had died when our brethren died before the LORD! Why have you brought the assembly of the LORD into this wilderness, that we should die here, both we and our cattle? And why have you made us come up out of Egypt, to bring us to this evil place? It is no place for grain, or figs, or vines, or pomegranates; and there is no water to drink." Then Moses and Aaron went from the presence of the assembly to the door of the tent of meeting, and fell on their faces. And the glory of the LORD appeared to them, and the LORD said to Moses, "Take the rod, and assemble the congregation, you and Aaron your brother, and tell the rock before their eyes to yield its water; so you shall bring water out of the rock for them; so you shall give drink to the congregation and their cattle." And Moses took the rod from before the LORD, as he commanded him.

And Moses and Aaron gathered the assembly together before the rock, and he said to them, "Hear now, you rebels; shall we bring forth water for you out of this rock?" And Moses lifted up his hand and struck the rock with his rod twice; and water came forth abundantly, and the congregation drank, and their cattle. And the LORD said to Moses and Aaron, "Because you did not believe in me, to sanctify me in the eyes of the people of Israel, therefore you shall not bring this assembly into the land which I have given them." These are the waters of Meribah, where the people of Israel contended with the LORD, and he showed himself holy among them. (Numbers 20:2-13.)

In both cases the people of Israel are about to start a riot: in our reading for today, Moses tells the Lord that he genuinely fears for his life. In both cases, Moses strikes the rock, and plenty of water comes out. Furthermore, in both cases the place is named "Meribah" after the strife that happened there.

In the first story—the one we read this Sunday—Moses strictly obeys the Lord. In the second story, God tells him to *command* the rock but he strikes the rock instead—twice. From his angry words beforehand, we get the impression that Moses had had it up to *here* with the people of Israel, and striking the rock twice suggests that he was pounding it angrily in an unholy display of bad temper. He also doesn't mention anything about God: rather, he seems to give himself and Aaron credit for bringing out the water.

God grants the water to his people both times, even though Moses has to suffer the penalty for his disobedience and lack of faith the second time. In the hot and arid climate of Palestine, clear running water to drink is a powerful image of life. In this story, the rock is at Horeb, which is another name for Sinai—the mountain where, shortly afterward, the Law would be given to the people of Israel. Just as water gives life to the people, so the Law would give life to the whole nation of Israel.

Because there are two stories of Moses striking the rock to bring forth water and because in both stories the place is called Meribah, some theologians think that the rock was actually the same rock and that it followed the Israelites through the desert. St. Paul sees this rock as a "type" or image of Christ—or perhaps something even stronger.

I want you to know, brethren, that our fathers were all under the cloud, and all passed through the sea, and all were baptized into Moses in the cloud and in the sea, and all ate the same supernatural food and all drank the same supernatural drink. For they drank from the supernatural Rock which followed them, and the Rock was Christ. (1 Corinthians 4:1-4.)

Paul says simply that the Rock was Christ. If we take him literally, he says that Christ was actually present in the desert with the Israelites, giving them running water to drink. And when we remember that "In the beginning was the Word" (John 1:1), that interpretation seems quite likely.

Wherever there is water in the Old Testament, the earliest Christians saw a figure of baptism. The Flood was a baptism; the crossing of the Red Sea was a baptism; the living water from the rock in the desert prefigures the water of baptism. There is more to our baptism than water but these events are foreshadowing of our baptism.

Second Reading: Romans 5:1-2, 5-8

When the Gospels tell us about Christian baptism, they make a strong distinction between it and the forms of baptism that came before. "I have baptized you with water; but he will baptize you with the Holy Spirit," said John the Baptist (Mark 1:8). Jesus told us, "Truly, truly, I say to you, unless one is born of water and the Spirit, he cannot enter the kingdom of God" (John 3:5).

In Christian baptism, water is absolutely essential for the sacrament. However, it is the coming of the Holy Spirit that makes Christian baptism different from any simple ritual cleansing.

As St. Paul says God's love is "poured into our hearts through the Holy Spirit." Our hope in Christ is not misplaced, because at baptism we received the Holy Spirit. We can be more than hopeful, in fact: we can be confident, as St. John Chrysostom told his congregation in the following passage;

Now, no one who has lived an upright life is not confident about things to come, though there are many of those who have been negligent who, feeling the burden of a bad conscience, wish there were neither judgment nor retribution. So does that mean our goods lie in hopes? Yes, in hopes—but not mere human hopes, which often slip away, and disappoint the one who hoped—as when someone who was expected to patronize him dies, or is changed though he lives. Our case is nothing like that: our hope is sure and immovable. For he who has made the promise ever lives, and we who are to enjoy of it, even if we should die, shall rise again. And there is absolutely nothing that can disappoint us, for we were not elated at random and pointlessly with unsound hopes.

—*St. John Chrysostom, Homily 9 on Romans*

This leads up to our Gospel reading, where we hear how Jesus himself brought hope to a particularly hopeless individual.

Gospel Reading: John 4:5-42

This Gospel reading is very detailed story by Gospel standards. All the Gospel writers were very economical with words: they told what needed to be told and added no unnecessary details. The fact that St. John gives so much space to this story indicates just how important he thought it was.

Why is it important? In order to understand we need to know a little bit about the historical background. As John says, "Jews have no dealings with Samaritans," and that was for complicated historical reasons. Samaritans have a long and fascinating history—a history that may at last be coming to an end within our own lifetimes.

After King Solomon died, the majority of Israel rebelled against his son Rehoboam and set up a kingdom in the north. Rehoboam kept Judah, the tribe of his ancestors, as well as the tiny tribe of Simeon and those members of the priestly tribe of Levi who lived within his borders. His kingdom, the southern third or so of the kingdom he inherited from his father, was known as Judah named for the tribe that made up the huge majority of its people. The rest of the tribes followed Jeroboam and formed the northern kingdom of Israel, whose capital was eventually placed at Samaria—a name that came to be applied to the whole kingdom, the way modern reporters say "Moscow" when they mean the Russian government.

Since the two kingdoms were often at war and barely tolerated each other even in peacetime, the people of Israel stopped going to the Temple in Jerusalem to worship. Instead, they worshiped at sacred sites within their own borders. The most sacred of all those sites is Mount Gerizim, which is still the Samaritans' holy place today.

The Assyrian Empire conquered the kingdom of Israel about 700 years before Christ. They forced the upper class of the population into exile and only the poorer classes were left to tend the land. The Assyrians then brought colonists from elsewhere in their vast empire to repopulate Israel. According to Jewish history, those colonists mixed with the remnants of the people of Israel to form the Samaritans.

Meanwhile, the kingdom of Judah held out against the Assyrians but fell to the Babylonians who had conquered Assyria and inherited the empire. The Jewish people ("Jewish" comes from the name "Judah") were exiled to Babylon but some were allowed to return to Judah when the Persians conquered the Babylonians. The books of Ezra and Nehemiah tell the story of their return from exile and in particular their conflicts with the people they found living there when they got back.

Jews regarded Samaritans as debased half-pagans who worshiped the Lord in the wrong way. Samaritans, on the other hand, believe that theirs is the true religion of Israel and that the Jews brought back a corrupted religion from Babylon.

You can see why the relations between Jews and Samaritans were filled with mutual hatred and distrust. Jews and Samaritans literally would not speak to each other. Jews going from Galilee to Jerusalem would cross the Jordan and go miles out of their way rather than walk through Samaritan territory.

Today, some of that mutual distrust still remains. There are fewer than 800 Samaritans left, almost all of them living around or near Mount Gerizim in the West Bank. In Jesus' time, there were close to a million Samaritans and people who thought of themselves as good Jews avoided every single one of them.

Within that context, we can see why it was astonishing to the disciples that Jesus was talking with this woman: not only was she female, she was also a Samaritan! Men don't talk to women in public and "Jews have no dealings with Samaritans"—those were two rules good Jewish men grew up with.

We need to examine what Jesus is saying when he and the Samaritan woman talk about "living water."

"If you knew the gift of God, and who it is that is saying to you, 'Give me a drink,' you would have asked him, and he would have given you living water." The woman said to him, "Sir, you have nothing to draw with, and the well is deep; where do you get that living water? Are you greater than our father Jacob, who gave us the well, and drank from it himself, and his sons, and his cattle?"

In their Aramaic language, as well as in Greek and Latin, "living water" is the common term for what we call "running water" or "fresh water"—good, clear, moving water like the water that came from the rock in the desert, as opposed to still or stagnant water. "That is commonly called living water which issues from a spring," St. Augustine explains; "that which is collected from rain in pools and cisterns is not called living water." At first, that kind of "living water" is what the Samaritan woman thinks Jesus is offering her.

The woman, however, being in suspense, says to him, "Sir, you have nothing to draw with, and the well is deep." See how she understood the "living water": it was simply the water which was in that fountain. "You would give me living water, and I carry that with which to draw, and you do not. The living water is here; how are you to give it me?" She understands it as something else, and taking it materially, she is knocking, so to speak, so that the Master may open up that which is closed. She was knocking in ignorance, not with earnest purpose; she is still an object of pity, not yet of instruction.   —*St. Augustine, Tractate 15 on John.*

The Samaritan woman only begins to understand that there's more to it when Jesus says, "Every one who drinks of this water will thirst again, but whoever drinks of the water that I shall give him will never thirst; the water that I shall give him will become in him a spring of water welling up to eternal life."

Even then, she still thinks in terms of the very practical and earthly business of trudging back and forth with a bucket: "Sir, give me this water, that I may not thirst, nor come here to draw."

We then learn even more about this Samaritan woman. We discover that she is the sort of woman her fellow Samaritans would probably shun. She has had five husbands and now she lives with a man who is not her husband. Jesus knows that she is a Samaritan and he knows her living conditions and yet it hasn't deterred him from talking to her.

She can see now that Jesus is a prophet and brings up the point of dispute that Samaritans never get a chance to talk about with Jewish teachers: "Our fathers worshiped on this mountain; and you say that in Jerusalem is the place where men ought to worship." But she must really be thinking, "Why are you, a Jew, talking to me?"

Jesus does not erase the *historical* difference between Jews and Samaritans. The prophets are right:

Jerusalem is the place of worship, at least for the time being. For the time is coming when the difference between Jew and Samaritan will be meaningless, because "the true worshipers will worship the Father in spirit and truth." The woman tells him she knows the Messiah is coming and then Jesus says an extraordinary thing: "I who speak to you am he."

It's extraordinary because this is the first time in John's Gospel where Jesus has actually told anyone that he is the Messiah. Whom does he tell? Not Peter, not "the disciple whom Jesus loved," not the Temple authorities but a Samaritan woman of dubious reputation.

Once he has told her, she can't keep the news to herself. She runs off—leaving the water jug that she had so laboriously filled—to tell everyone she knows to come see this marvelous man. Can he really be the Messiah?

Observe her zeal and wisdom. She came to draw water, and when she had happened upon the true Well, then she despised the material one—teaching us even by this trifling instance when we are listening to spiritual matters to overlook the things of this life, and make no account of them. For what the apostles did, this woman did too, according to her ability. When they were called, they left their nets; she of her own accord, without the command of any, leaves her water pot, and winged by joy performs the office of Evangelists. And she calls not one or two, as did Andrew and Philip, but having aroused a whole city and people, so brought them to him.

Observe too how prudently she speaks; she said not, Come and see the Christ, but with the same condescension by which Christ had netted her she draws the men to him; "Come," she says, "see a

man who told me all that ever I did." She was not ashamed to say that "he told me all that ever I did." Yet she could have said something else—"Come, see someone who prophesies." But when the soul is inflamed with holy fire, it looks then to nothing earthly, neither to glory nor to shame, but belongs to one thing alone, the flame which occupies it.

"Can this be the Christ?" Observe again here the great wisdom of the woman; she neither declared the fact plainly, nor was she silent, for she desired not to bring them in by her own assertion, but to make them to share in this opinion by hearing Him; which rendered her words more readily acceptable to them. Yet he had not told all her life to her, only from what had been said she was persuaded that he knew the rest. Nor did she say, "Come, believe," but, "Come, see"; a gentler expression than the other, and one that attracted them more.

Do you see the wisdom of the woman? She knew—she knew certainly—that, having only tasted that Well, they would be affected in the same way she was. Yet any one of the grosser sort would have concealed the reproof which Jesus had given; but she parades her own life, and brings it forward before all, so as to attract and capture all.   —St. John Chrysostom, *Homily 34 on the Gospel of John.*

If St. John Chrysostom is right about this woman's wisdom, then it certainly paid off. The people of the city were indeed attracted to see for themselves, and once they had seen for themselves they believed—not because of what the woman had told them but because Christ had the words of eternal life.

Lenten Moment

Why did we spend so much time thinking about baptism today?

The overwhelming majority of Catholics today were baptized in infancy. Still, many parishes will see some adult converts come to be baptized. By ancient tradition, they are welcomed into the Church at Easter Vigil, when the long season of repentance is over. In the early centuries of the Church, converts were streaming in by the countless thousands, and Lent was very obviously a season of preparation for baptism.

The early Christians took baptism far more seriously than most of us do today. It was common for converts—like the emperor Constantine—to delay their baptism until they were near death. Why? Because they knew that baptism washes away sins, and they thought it was a very serious thing to sin after baptism. They didn't trust themselves to keep from sinning for years and years, so they wanted to die with a clean slate. When converts were baptized, they spent the season of Lent preparing by repentance and fasting, while they were receiving religious instruction from the bishop.

Today most of the people in a Catholic church during Lent are already baptized. Lent is still a time of repentance and preparation and especially a time when we reflect on our own sinful nature and the wonderful gift of baptism that heals what is bruised in every one of us.

Catechism Connections

- For information on how faith seeks understanding see CCC 158

- To see more on Faith as an entirely free gift from God see CCC162

- For more about the Sacraments and Faith see CCC1125

- For understanding about the Holy Spirit as the living water see CCC 2652

- For an explanation of how the first commandment embraces faith, hope and charity, see CCC 208

- For deeper understanding about the spirit of Christ in the fullness of time see CCC 728

Rome to Home

This year, on this Third Sunday of Lent, the liturgy again presents one of the most beautiful and profound passages of the Bible: the dialogue between Jesus and the Samaritan woman (cf. Jn 4: 5-42). St Augustine, of whom I am speaking extensively in the Wednesday Catecheses, was justifiably fascinated by this narrative, and he made a memorable comment on it. It is impossible to give a brief explanation of the wealth of this Gospel passage. One must read and meditate on it personally, identifying oneself with that woman who, one day like so many other days, went to draw water from the well and found Jesus there, sitting next to it, "tired from the journey" in the midday heat. "Give me a drink," he said, leaving her very surprised: it was in fact completely out of the ordinary that a Jew would speak to a Samaritan woman, and all the more so to a stranger. But the woman's bewilderment was destined to increase. Jesus spoke of a "living water" able to quench her thirst and become in her "a spring of water welling up to eternal life"; in addition, he demonstrated that he knew her personal life; he revealed that the hour has come to adore the one true God in spirit and truth; and lastly, he entrusted her with something extremely rare: that he is the Messiah.

All this began from the real and notable experience of thirst. The theme of thirst runs throughout John's Gospel: from the meeting with the Samaritan woman to the great prophecy during the feast of Tabernacles (Jn 7: 37-38), even to the Cross, when Jesus, before he dies, said to fulfil the Scriptures: "I thirst" (Jn 19: 28). Christ's thirst is an entranceway to the mystery of God, who became thirsty to satisfy our thirst, just as he became poor to make us rich (cf. II Cor 8: 9). Yes, God thirsts for our faith and our love. As a good and merciful father, he wants our total, possible good, and this good is he himself. The Samaritan woman, on the other hand, represents the existential dissatisfaction of one who does not find what he seeks. She had "five husbands" and now she lives with another man; her going to and from the well to draw water expresses a repetitive and resigned life. However, everything changes for her that day, thanks to the conversation with the Lord Jesus, who upsets her to the point that she leaves her pitcher of water and runs to tell the villagers: "Come, see a man who told me all that I ever did. Can this be the Christ?" (Jn 4: 29).

Dear brothers and sisters, like the Samaritan woman, let us also open our hearts to listen trustingly to God's Word in order to encounter Jesus who reveals his love to us and tells us: "I who speak to you am he" (Jn 4: 26), the Messiah, your Saviour. May Mary, the first and most perfect disciple of the Word made flesh, obtain this gift for us.

—*Pope Benedict XVI, Angelus, February 24, 2008.*

Voices of the Saints

Only let us not be condemned for frivolity by asking for little, and for what is unworthy of the Giver. Blessed is he from whom Jesus asks drink, as he did from that Samaritan woman, and gives a well of water springing up unto eternal life.

—*St. Gregory Nazianzen, Oration 40, 27.*

Study Questions

1. In today's first reading, what does Moses ask of God and why? What is God's response?

2. In our Second Reading according to St. Paul, why do we have reason to hope?

3. In this week's Gospel reading what does Jesus ask the Samaritan woman for, what was her response and why?

4. What extraordinary revelation does Jesus make first to the Samaritan woman and why is it extraordinary that he revealed it to a Samaritan woman?

5. How did the disciples react to finding Jesus talking with a Samaritan woman?

6. According to the Gospel of John, why did "many more" of the Samaritans of that city believe in Christ?

Notes

Week 4: Darkness and Light

Darkness and light, blindness and sight—these are our themes today. Samuel the prophet has to learn that "the LORD sees not as man sees; man looks on the outward appearance, but the LORD looks on the heart." St. Paul urges us to wake from the darkness and live in the light of Christ. The Gospel tells us how Jesus healed a man born blind—and how the Pharisees showed themselves to be blind, even though they were born with sight.

One theme that runs through all three readings is sight: we do not really see until we see the world the way God sees it. Sinners live in darkness. Our human judgment fails to see the inner truth. And a blind man with faith sees better than a Pharisee who will not believe.

Another theme that runs through the today's readings is baptism. It may not be obvious at first but notice how important "anointing" and "washing" are in the Old Testament and Gospel readings. With the anointing of David the Holy Spirit comes to him. Likewise, Jesus tells the man born blind to wash in the pool of Siloam. As we know, Lent is a season of preparation for baptism; today's readings are telling us what our baptism really means. Even though most of the congregation you find in a Catholic church will have already been baptized, our lives are still a cycle of sin, repentance, and forgiveness.

Old Testament Reading: 1 Samuel 16:1, 6-7, 10-13

The LORD said to Samuel, "How long will you grieve over Saul, seeing I have rejected him from being king over Israel? Fill your horn with oil, and go; I will send you to Jesse the Bethlehemite, for I have provided for myself a king among his sons." When they came, he looked on Eliab and thought, "Surely the LORD's anointed is before him." But the LORD said to Samuel, "Do not look on his appearance or on the height of his stature, because I have rejected him; for the LORD sees not as man sees; man looks on the outward appearance, but the LORD looks on the heart." And Jesse made seven of his sons pass before Samuel. And Samuel said to Jesse, "The LORD has not chosen these." And Samuel said to Jesse, "Are all your sons here?" And he said, "There remains yet the youngest, but behold, he is keeping the sheep." And Samuel said to Jesse, "Send and fetch him; for we will not sit down till he comes here." And he sent, and brought him in. Now he was ruddy, and had beautiful eyes, and was handsome. And the LORD said, "Arise, anoint him; for this is he." Then Samuel took the horn of oil, and anointed him in the midst of his brothers; and the Spirit of the LORD came mightily upon David from that day forward. And Samuel rose up, and went to Ramah.

New Testament Reading: Ephesians 5:8-14

For once you were darkness, but now you are light in the Lord; walk as children of light (for the fruit of light is found in all that is good and right and true), and try to learn what is pleasing to the Lord. Take no part in the unfruitful works of darkness, but instead expose them. For it is a shame even to speak of the things that they do in secret; but when anything is exposed by the light it becomes visible, for anything that becomes visible is light. Therefore it is said, "Awake, O sleeper, and arise from the dead, and Christ shall give you light."

Gospel Reading: John 9:1-41

As he passed by, he saw a man blind from his birth. And his disciples asked him, "Rabbi, who sinned, this man or his parents, that he was born blind?" Jesus answered, "It was not that this man sinned, or his parents, but that the works of God might be made manifest in him. We must work the works of him who sent me, while it is day; night comes, when no one can work. As long as I am in the world, I am the light of the world." As he said this, he spat on the ground and made clay of the spittle and anointed the man's eyes with the clay, saying to him, "Go, wash in the pool of Siloam" (which means Sent). So he went and washed and came back seeing. The neighbors and those who had seen him before as a beggar, said, "Is not this the man who used to sit and beg?" Some said, "It is he"; others said, "No, but he is like him." He said, "I am the man." They said to him, "Then how were your eyes opened?" He answered, "The man called Jesus made clay and anointed my eyes and said to me, 'Go to Siloam and wash'; so I went and washed and received my sight." They said to him, "Where is he?" He said, "I do not know." They brought to the Pharisees the man who had formerly been blind. Now it was a sabbath day when Jesus made the clay and opened his eyes. The Pharisees again asked him how he had received his sight. And he said to them, "He put clay on my eyes, and I washed, and I see." Some of the Pharisees said, "This man is not from God, for he does not keep the sabbath." But others said, "How can a man who is a sinner do such signs?" There was a division among them. So they again said to the blind man, "What do you say about him, since he has opened your eyes?" He said, "He is a prophet." The Jews did not believe that he had been blind and had received his sight, until they called the parents of the man who had received his sight, and asked them, "Is this your son, who you say was born blind? How then does he now see?" His parents answered, "We know that this is our son, and that he was born blind; but how he now sees we do not know, nor do we know who opened his eyes. Ask him; he is of age, he will speak for himself." His parents said this because they feared the Jews, for the Jews had already agreed that if any one should confess him to be Christ, he was to be put out of the synagogue. Therefore his parents said, "He is of age, ask him." So for the second time they called the man who had been blind, and said to him, "Give God the praise; we know that this man is a sinner." He answered, "Whether he is a sinner, I do not know; one thing I know, that though I was blind, now I see." They said to him, "What did he do to you? How did he open your eyes?" He answered them, "I have told you already, and you would not listen. Why do you want to hear it again? Do you too want to become his disciples?" And they reviled him, saying, "You are his disciple, but we are disciples of Moses. We know that God has spoken to Moses, but as for this man, we do not know where he comes from." The man answered, "Why, this is a marvel! You do not know where he comes from, and yet he opened my eyes. We know that God does not listen to sinners, but if any one is a worshiper of God and does his will, God listens to him. Never since the world began has it been heard that any one opened the eyes of a man born blind. If this man were not from God, he could do nothing." They answered him, "You were born in utter sin, and would you teach us?" And they cast him out. Jesus heard that they had cast him out, and having found him he said, "Do you believe in the Son of man?" He answered, "And who is he, sir, that I may believe in him?" 37 Jesus said to him, "You have seen him, and it is he who speaks to you." He said, "Lord, I believe"; and he worshipped him. Jesus said, "For judgment I came into this world, that those who do not see may see, and that those who see may become blind." Some of the Pharisees near him heard this, and they said to him, "Are we also blind?" Jesus said to them, "If you were blind, you would have no guilt; but now that you say, 'We see,' your guilt remains."

Points to Ponder

1 Samuel 16:1, 6-7, 10-13

When the Israelites demanded a king, so that they could be like all the other nations, the Lord warned them, through the prophet Samuel, that they wouldn't like kings much. Kings raise your taxes, draft you into the army, and conscript you for public-works projects. The Israelites stubbornly insisted, however, so the Lord directed Samuel to make Saul king over Israel. Saul had been taller and more handsome than anyone (see 1 Samuel 9:2). He looked every inch a king. He was just what the Israelites had in mind: someone impressive to stand in front of the army to appear royal and terrifying their enemies.

Saul, however, proved a disobedient servant, and the Lord told Samuel to go anoint one of Jesse's sons as king to replace Saul. This is where our story today picks up.

"The LORD sees not as man sees; man looks on the outward appearance, but the LORD looks on the heart." One by one the sons of Jesse parade by and Samuel is all in favor of the tall and kingly ones—the ones who look like worthy successors to Saul. However, God hadn't chosen any of them.

Instead, God has chosen David, who looks insignificant and is so little regarded by his family that no one had even bothered to call him in from the fields. We aren't told whether Samuel had revealed the purpose of his errand to Jesse but surely Jesse knows that something very important was about to happen to one of his sons. Samuel is universally known as the judge who anointed Saul—the king-maker with a direct line to God. If he's in town with his anointing horn and he wants to see your sons, you have to start imagining great things for your boys. So it's clear that Jesse thinks his son David is completely out of the running.

Both Jesse and Samuel are judging by appearances: David doesn't look like a king. God, however, sees David's heart and in spite of Samuel's own private opinions about what a king should look like he ends up calling David in from the fields and making him king in place of Saul.

The ceremony that makes a king is anointing; Samuel has his oil at the ready to anoint the one God will show him. This anointing was a very powerful thing in the eyes of the faithful: it meant that God approved the king who would be the leader of the nation. Saul had been anointed by Samuel (see 1 Samuel 10:1).

You might have expected that, since David knew he was anointed to replace Saul as king of Israel, he would have taken steps to get rid of Saul right away. Instead, he served Saul faithfully, even when the inevitable civil war came because of Saul's mad jealousy. Twice during the conflict David had Saul in his power and twice he spared Saul's life. Why? Saul was the Lord's anointed. That's how important the anointing was.

The first time, Saul had gone into a cave alone "to relieve himself" (since public rest rooms were hard to find in those days). It happened to be a cave where David and his men were hiding, and David's men wanted to kill Saul and put an end to the civil war but David would not permit it. Instead, he sneaked up behind Saul and cut off a piece of his garment, just to prove how close he had been—but he even felt guilty about that.

"He said to his men, "The LORD forbid that I should do this thing to my lord, the LORD'S anointed, to put forth my hand against him, seeing he is the LORD'S anointed." So David persuaded his men with these words, and did not permit them to attack Saul."

—1 Samuel 24:6-7

The next time David had Saul in his power was when Saul and the men around him were fast asleep. Once again, David's companion wants to kill Saul and be done with it. But once again the fact that Saul is the Lord's anointed is an insuperable objection for David.

"So David and Abishai went to the army by night; and there lay Saul sleeping within the encampment, with his spear stuck in the ground at his head; and Abner and the army lay around him. Then said Abishai to David, "God has given your enemy into your hand this day; now therefore let me pin him to the earth with one stroke of the spear, and I will not strike him twice." But David said to Abishai, "Do not destroy him; for who can put forth his hand against the LORD'S anointed, and be guiltless?" And David said, "As the LORD lives, the LORD will smite him; or his day shall come to die; or he shall go down into battle and perish. The LORD forbid that I should put forth my hand against the LORD'S anointed; but take now the spear that is at his head, and the jar of water, and let us go."

—*1 Samuel 26:7-11.*

Saul is holy because he was anointed by God's prophet, even if he is also a tyrant and sometimes a madman. David respects that holiness even though he knows that he himself was anointed—by the same prophet—to replace Saul as king of Israel.

The word in Hebrew that means "the anointed one" is usually transliterated "messiah" in English. The Greek equivalent is "christ" ("*christos*"). The title "Christ" that we give to Jesus of Nazareth is his title by virtue of being King of Israel: he is the Lord's Anointed.

Aphrahat, a Syriac writer of the early 300s, made a long list of parallels between David the anointed and Jesus the anointed:

David was anointed by Samuel to be king instead of Saul who had sinned; and Jesus was anointed by John to be High Priest instead of the priests, the ministers of the Law.

David was persecuted after his anointing; and Jesus was persecuted after his anointing.

David reigned first over one tribe only, and afterwards over all Israel; and Jesus reigned from the beginning over the few who believed on him, and in the end he will reign over all the world.

Samuel anointed David when he was thirty years old; and Jesus when about thirty years old received the imposition of the hand from John.

David wedded two daughters of the king; and Jesus wedded two daughters of kings, the congregation of the People and the congregation of the Gentiles.

David repaid good to Saul his enemy; and Jesus taught us to pray for our enemies [Luke 6:28].

David was the heart of God [1 Samuel 13:14], and Jesus was the Son of God.

David received the kingdom of Saul his persecutor; and Jesus received the kingdom of Israel his persecutor.

David wept with dirges over Saul his enemy when he died; and Jesus wept over Jerusalem, his persecutor, which was to be laid waste.

David handed over the kingdom to Solomon, and was gathered to his people; and Jesus handed over the keys to Simon, and ascended and returned to him who sent him.

For David's sake, sins were forgiven to his posterity; and for Jesus' sake sins are forgiven to the nations.
                                                                    —*Aphrahat, Demonstration 21, 13*

Ephesians 5:8-14

St. Paul makes a sharp contrast between *light* and *darkness*. Darkness is sin; light comes from Christ, and it dispels the shadows of sin.

Before we were converted to Christ we were in "darkness". Now that we have the light of Christ in us, we should be able to recognize sin for what it is, "exposing" it to the light. If we do what is pleasing to the Lord, then we are living as "children of light."

St. John Chrysostom explains that the *sleeper*—the one who must *arise from the dead*—is the sinner.

By the *sleeper* and the *dead*, he means whoever is in sin; for the sinner both puts out loathsome odors like the dead, and is inactive like one that is asleep, and like him he sees nothing, but is dreaming, and forming fancies and illusions.... Leave sin, and you will be able to see Christ. "For every one who does evil hates the light, and does not come to the light" [John 3:20]. Then whoever does not do evil comes to the light.

Now he is not saying this with reference to the unbelievers only, for many of the faithful stick to wickedness as much as the unbelievers—in fact, some do it far more. Therefore we must also exclaim to them, "Awake, O sleeper, and arise from the dead, and Christ shall give you light." It is fitting, too, to say to them, "God is not God of the dead, but of the living" [Matthew 22:32]. If he is not the God of the dead, let us live!
                                                                    —*St. John Chrysostom, Homily 18 on Ephesians.*

What does it really mean to walk as children of light? Our reading today is short and gives us the abstract principle. However, St. Paul did not stick to abstractions: he began with very concrete instructions.

Therefore be imitators of God, as beloved children. And walk in love, as Christ loved us and gave himself up for us, a fragrant offering and sacrifice to God. But fornication and all impurity or covetousness must not even be named among you, as is fitting among saints. Let there be no filthiness, nor silly talk, nor levity, which are not fitting; but instead let there be thanksgiving. Be sure of this, that no fornicator or impure man, or one who is covetous (that is, an idolater), has any inheritance in the kingdom of Christ and of God. Let no one deceive you with empty words, for it is because of these things that the wrath of God comes upon the sons of disobedience. —*Ephesians 5:1-6.*

That is what introduces the passage we read today. After it, Paul goes on with more specifics:

And do not get drunk with wine, for that is debauchery; but be filled with the Spirit, addressing one another in psalms and hymns and spiritual songs, singing and making melody to the Lord with all your heart, always and for everything giving thanks in the name of our Lord Jesus Christ to God the Father. —*Ephesians 5:18-20.*

Living in the light is living a life of joy and thanksgiving, not drunkenness or "filthiness." In fact Paul seems to suggest being "filled with the spirit" as an alternative to drunken debauchery: a life of real and permanent joy, rather than the false and temporary elation that comes with too much wine and "impurity." He is telling us what is pleasing to God—but what is pleasing to God is, after all, only what is good for us.

John 9:1-41

Today's Gospel reading makes an ironic distinction between "seeing" and "blindness" that reminds us of the lesson Samuel had to learn in the Old Testament reading: the way the world sees things is not the way God sees them. The man who is physically blind can "see" better—even before he is healed—than the authority figures who have physical sight but can't see beyond their prejudices and the bare words of the Law.

It was a common belief in Jesus' time that any physical disability or misfortune was a punishment for sin. If a child was born with a disability, like the man "blind from his birth" in today's Gospel, then it was a punishment for the sins of his parents.

Certainly not all Jews held this belief. The prophet Ezekiel had already pronounced God's word against it:

The word of the LORD came to me again: "What do you mean by repeating this proverb concerning the land of Israel, 'The fathers have eaten sour grapes, and the children's teeth are set on edge'? 3 As I live, says the Lord GOD, this proverb shall no more be used by you in Israel. Behold, all souls are mine; the soul of the father as well as the soul of the son is mine: the soul that sins shall die.... The son shall not suffer for the iniquity of the father, nor the father suffer for the iniquity of the son; the righteousness of the righteous shall be upon himself, and the wickedness of the wicked shall be upon himself." —*Ezekiel 18:1-4, 20*

The story we hear this Sunday shows us, it was a common belief that a man born blind was "born in utter sin."

Jesus' disciples have apparently been learning something from their Teacher. They recognize at least that the common belief poses a problem. How could the man born blind be punished for his own sins if he was born blind before he had a chance to sin? And if his parents were the sinners, then how is it fair that he should be punished?

Nevertheless, they're not ready to break out of the old model that says misfortune is always a punishment for sin. So they ask Jesus to sort out the difficulty for them and "Jesus answered, "It was not that this man sinned, or his parents, but that the works of God might be made manifest in him." Jesus then healed the man, so that he can see.

Does that mean that an innocent man had to suffer so that Jesus could teach us a lesson? St. John Chrysostom tackled that question, telling his congregation that they needed to rethink their idea of what was a bad thing. The only bad thing in life is sin. Blindness, which ordinary people would think was a misfortune, actually led to good for the man born blind.

But here we have another difficulty, if without this man's punishment it was not possible that the glory of God should be shown. However, it is not said that it was *impossible*—for it *was* possible—but, "that it might be manifested" even in this man.

What, says someone, did he suffer wrong for the glory of God?

But tell me, what wrong did he suffer? What if God had never willed to produce him at all?

But I say that he even received benefit from his blindness, since he recovered the sight of the eyes within. What good did the eyes of the "Jews" do them? They earned a heavier punishment, because they were blinded even while they saw. And what injury did this man have from his blindness? For by means of it he recovered sight.

> Just as the evils of the present life are not evils, so neither are the good things good; sin alone is an evil, but blindness is not an evil. And he who had brought this man from not being into being had also power to leave him as he was.
>
> —*St. John Chrysostom, Homily 56 on the Gospel of John.*

So the man receives his sight—but that's only half the story. It is unusual but in this reading we are given a long and detailed account of the aftermath of one of Jesus' miracles.

It goes pretty much the way we might expect it to go if it happened today. At first people don't believe it's the same man at all; then they doubt his story. "The Jews" begin a long interrogation that exasperates the poor man.

It's important for us to remember that, when John says "the Jews," he always means the Jewish authorities or people like the Pharisees who set themselves up as authorities on the Law of Moses. He doesn't mean anything like "the Jewish race." By ancestry, John himself was a Jew; the blind man's parents who spoke cautiously "because they feared the Jews" were Jews; Christ and all his disciples were Jews. The reason it's important for us to remember that is because some people who call themselves Christians have used John's opposition to "the Jews" as an excuse for racism. The term "the Jews" obviously has nothing to do with race in John's Gospel; it is simply John's word for the forces of the Jewish establishment that arrayed themselves against Jesus.

We tend to give the Pharisees a bad reputation, as if they were all enemies of Christ, they are not. In this case, some of the Pharisees are open-minded. Many of them were sympathetic to him and a large number became his disciples. St. Paul, after all, was a Pharisee. We tend to forget about the sympathetic Pharisees because the Gospels record so many of Jesus' disputes with Pharisees who are not. Here we meet some of the sympathizers: "How can a man who is a sinner do such signs?" they ask.

Others, however—the ones John will call "the Jews" in the rest of the reading—are skeptical. They are not sure that a miracle has happened at all, and if it has happened, it was done on the Sabbath, which is a violation of their interpretation of the Law. They interrogate the formerly blind man and then they bring his parents in for questioning. Obviously the interrogators are people with power and influence, since the parents are afraid of offending them; they only reply that their son can speak for himself.

And he does speak for himself. He does not know who this Jesus is but he does know what he himself has experienced. "Whether he is a sinner, I do not know; one thing I know, that though I was blind, now I see."

His interrogators refuse to accept that simple answer and the fact that they can't think of a reply to it seems to make them angrier. But the formerly blind man is ready to believe. He meets Jesus again, and confesses him as the Christ. And then Jesus gives him one of those infuriating paradoxes that annoyed the Pharisees so much: "For judgment I came into this world, that those who do not see may see, and that those who see may become blind."

That catches the ears of some of the unsympathetic Pharisees, who sarcastically ask, "Are we also blind?" Jesus' reply to them tells them what kind of sight he's really talking about: not the sight of the eyes, but the willingness to accept God working in the world. "If you were blind, you would have no guilt; but now that you say, 'We see,' your guilt remains." It isn't blindness of the eyes that's the problem: it's blindness of the mind. Blindness of the eyes is nobody's fault—that was the answer to the disciples' question. But if you willingly shut yourself off from the truth, you have no one to blame but yourself.

Now that we have heard what Jesus said, we should turn our attention to what he did. One of the striking things about this healing is how *physical* it is. Jesus could easily have simply opened the man's eyes and he would have been healed. Instead, Jesus uses physical clay and tells the man to wash in the pool of Siloam.

This is the way sacraments work. We are not spirits trapped inside material bodies, ghosts in a machine: the material is as much who we are as the spiritual. We believe in the resurrection of the body, not simply in the persistence of the soul. And God sends his grace to us through material means showing that grace comes to the whole person, not just the spirit.

In baptism, we use water and holy oil to signify the coming of the Spirit, just as David was anointed with oil and the man born blind washed in the pool of Siloam. The material signs show the spiritual change.

Lenten Moment

Today we wrestle explicitly with the nature of sin.

On the one hand, Jesus tells his disciples very directly that neither the man born blind nor his parents sinned in any way that caused the man's blindness. That doesn't mean they weren't sinners but that the blindness wasn't caused by their sin specifically.

On the other hand, Genesis tells us that *all* misfortune in this world is ultimately caused by sin (see Genesis 3)—the sin we know as the Fall, when our first parents disobeyed God. Since then, life has been full of misfortune, sickness, and death. It was easy—and still is—for many people to identify a particular misfortune as a sign of a particular sin but the Scriptures tell us that the world doesn't work that way. As Ecclesiastes notes, the wicked often prosper as well as the good and the good, as we certainly see in Job, may suffer greatly in spite of their innocence.

Misfortune and illness can lead us closer to God, by reminding us of the need for repentance and purification. In the season of Lent especially we recall our need to repent, and God's infinite willingness to accept our repentance. In that way, the things we at first considered misfortunes may turn out not to be misfortunes at all.

The Fathers of the Church agree that in a mysterious way, a way we will never completely understand until the end of time, the world is *better* because of the Fall than it would have been without it. Evil is finite, but God's goodness is infinite. Even when we have to endure misfortunes brought on by our own sin, we can have faith that God remembers us and he is preparing a blessing for us greater than anything we can imagine.

Catechism Connections

- To understand better what it means for Jesus Christ to be the "Anointed One," see CCC 436-440.

- When was Christ "anointed"? See CCC 486.

- On the struggle between light and darkness, see CCC 1706-1707.

- To understand how illness and infirmity can lead us toward God, see CCC 1500-1501.

- To understand the meaning of Christ's miracles of healing, see CCC 1503-1505.

- For a sympathetic view of the Pharisees as a group, see CCC 578-579.

Rome to Home

Let us think about the experience of the blind man. He has not yet seen Jesus, he can only hear his voice and feel the Lord's fingers anointing his eyes. But he "went and washed and came back seeing" (Ibid. 9:7). Imagine his joy and his surprise as he looks at the world for the first time! The people standing round want to know how he has been cured. He tells them that it was done by "the man called Jesus" (Ibid. 9:11). But when they ask where Jesus is, the man has no answer. He has to admit: "I do not know" (Ibid 9:12). The man born blind has already received a great gift from the Lord, but a lot must happen before he will actually see Jesus and fully believe in him. First, he must resist the opposition of the Pharisees. Then, even his parents were afraid, and defended him only halfheartedly. The cured man does not yet have a full answer to the accusations made against Christ. He has only one argument, the fact that Jesus has cured him. "One thing I know, that though I was blind, now I see" (Jn. 9:25). He has one certainty, that Jesus is a good man, a prophet: "If this man were not from God, he could do nothing" (Ibid. 9:33).

Seeing that he publicly defended Jesus, the Pharisees "cast him out" (Ibid. 9:34). The blind man was now free to follow Christ, but he was also beginning to pay the price of discipleship. Then the Gospel tells us something very beautiful: "Jesus heard that they had cast him out" (Ibid. 9:35). The Lord never loses contact with his followers. He never abandons them. When they are alone and lost, he searches for them. That is the work of the Good Shepherd and of all those who take the place of the Chief Shepherd in the life of the Church. Jesus looked for the man whom he had cured, "and having found him he said: 'Do you believe in the Son of man?' " (Ibid.). Here we come to the heart of the Gospel message. *Nda ngom ngen: li di largte gi Yesu di wah chi ndaw u katolic yi neka chi rew mi tei (chi Gambia tei).* (Do you believe? This is the same question that Jesus addresses to the Catholic young people of The Gambia today). Is your faith in Jesus Christ, the Son of God and the Son of Mary, strong enough to give meaning and direction to your lives? To lead you out of fear and loneliness: To fill you with an ardent desire to serve his Kingdom and make it present in your own lives, in your families, in society?

Remember, the man has not yet seen Jesus with open eyes. But his heart is full of the desire to know the one who has done this great thing for him. He asks: "Who is he, sir, that I may believe in him?" (Ibid. 9:36). And then comes the great moment when Jesus reveals himself: "It is he who speaks to you" (Ibid. 9:37). When we are open, the light of Christ penetrates our hearts. When we discover him as the Way and the Truth and the Life, we are transformed (Cf. Jn. 14:6). God's truth teaches us wisdom; his love fills us with certainty, and with a great desire to do what he wants of us, and to share our discovery with others so that they too may have the marvellous experience of meeting the Lord. The cured man professes his faith: "Lord, I believe" (Ibid 9:38). At this moment he worships Jesus and a whole new world opens up before him. He enters into a new relationship with God. He will never again doubt God's unique love for him. He will adapt his life in every way to the will of God, to the following of Christ, to working for the coming of God's Kingdom in the heart of everyone he meets. *Yesu angi len di o' tei chi sen ngom.* (Jesus is calling you to just such an encounter of faith).

—*Pope John Paul II, Address in Banjul, February 23, 1992*

Voices of the Saints

"Faith is to believe what you do not see; the reward of this faith is to see what you believe."

—*St. Augustine*

Study Questions

1. What Christian sacraments resemble the anointing of kings in ancient Israel? What do all these ceremonies have in common? (Read 1 Samuel 16:19 carefully, noting both the anointing and its effect.)

2. How do we "expose" the works of darkness? How can we do that and still keep Christ's commandment, "Judge not, that you be not judged" (Matthew 7:1)?

3. According to our New Testament reading what does St. Paul say about how living a truly Christian life can be an alternative to drunkenness?

4. How are the works of God made manifest in the man born blind and in our neighbors today who have to deal with blindness or other disabilities? What part do we have to play in making the works of God manifest in them?

5. Why is it important for the blind man to wash himself in Siloam? (see CCC 1214-1216)

6. If neither his sin nor his parents' is the problem that made the man blind, why does Jesus insist on a ritual purification?

Lent Cycle A

Week 5: Resurrection

Introduction

Resurrection is our theme today, a theme that runs clearly through all three readings. Christians believe not just that the soul is immortal but that there will be a *resurrection of the body*. Ezekiel brings the word of the Lord promising to open the graves and raise the dead. St. Paul tells us that, though sin makes our bodies dead, Christ makes them live again. Finally, the Gospel tells the story of Lazarus, whom Jesus raised from the dead in a preview of the final resurrection.

Our Psalm today is the famous cry "out of the depths" (The "De profundis"). Although the Psalmist may be conscious of having sinned deeply, yet he also knows that "there is forgiveness with you." The Lord will redeem Israel even if nothing is left of Israel but dry bones.

Old Testament reading: Ezekiel 37:12-14

Therefore prophesy, and say to them, Thus says the Lord GOD: Behold, I will open your graves, and raise you from your graves, O my people; and I will bring you home into the land of Israel. And you shall know that I am the LORD, when I open your graves, and raise you from your graves, O my people. And I will put my Spirit within you, and you shall live, and I will place you in your own land; then you shall know that I, the LORD, have spoken, and I have done it, says the LORD.

New Testament reading: Romans 8:8-11

And those who are in the flesh cannot please God. But you are not in the flesh, you are in the Spirit, if in fact the Spirit of God dwells in you. Any one who does not have the Spirit of Christ does not belong to him. But if Christ is in you, although your bodies are dead because of sin, your spirits are alive because of righteousness. If the Spirit of him who raised Jesus from the dead dwells in you, he who raised Christ Jesus from the dead will give life to your mortal bodies also through his Spirit which dwells in you.

Gospel reading: John 11:1-45

Now a certain man was ill, Lazarus of Bethany, the village of Mary and her sister Martha. It was Mary who anointed the Lord with ointment and wiped his feet with her hair, whose brother Lazarus was ill. So the sisters sent to him, saying, "Lord, he whom you love is ill." But when Jesus heard it he said, "This illness is not unto death; it is for the glory of God, so that the Son of God may be glorified by means of it." Now Jesus loved Martha and her sister and Lazarus. So when he heard that he was ill, he stayed two days longer in the place where he was. Then after this he said to the disciples, "Let us go into Judea again." The disciples said to him, "Rabbi, the Jews were but now seeking to stone you, and are you going there again?" Jesus answered, "Are there not twelve hours in the day? If any one walks in the day, he does not stumble, because he sees the light of this world. But if any one walks in the night, he stumbles, because the light is not in him." Thus he spoke, and then he said to them, "Our friend Lazarus has fallen asleep, but I go to awake him out of sleep." The disciples said to him, "Lord, if he has fallen asleep, he will recover." Now Jesus had spoken of his death, but they thought that he meant taking rest in sleep. Then Jesus told them plainly, "Lazarus is dead; and for your sake I am glad that I was not there, so that you may believe. But let us go to him." Thomas, called the Twin, said to his fellow disciples, "Let us also go, that we may die with him." Now when Jesus came, he found that Lazarus had already been in the tomb four days. Bethany was near Jerusalem, about two miles off, and many of the Jews had come to Martha and Mary to console them concerning their brother. When Martha heard that Jesus was coming, she went and met him, while Mary sat in the house. Martha said to Jesus, "Lord, if you had been here, my brother would not have died. And even now I know that whatever you ask from God, God will give you." Jesus said to her, "Your brother will rise again." Martha said to him, "I know that he will rise again in the resurrection at the last day." Jesus said to her, "I am the resurrection and the life; he who believes in me, though he die, yet shall he live, and whoever lives and believes in me shall never die. Do you believe this?" She said to him, "Yes, Lord; I believe that you are the Christ, the Son of God, he who is coming into the world." When she had said this, she went and called her sister Mary, saying quietly, "The Teacher is here and is calling for you." And when she heard it, she rose quickly and went to him. Now Jesus had not yet come to the village, but was still in the place where Martha had met him. When the Jews who were with her in the house, consoling her, saw Mary rise quickly and go out, they followed her, supposing that she was going to the tomb to weep there. Then Mary, when she came where Jesus was and saw him, fell at his feet, saying to him, "Lord, if you had been here, my brother would not have died." When Jesus saw her weeping, and the Jews who came with her also weeping, he was deeply moved in spirit and troubled; and he said, "Where have you laid him?" They said to him, "Lord, come and see." Jesus wept. So the Jews said, "See how he loved him!" But some of them said, "Could not he who opened the eyes of the blind man have kept this man from dying?" Then Jesus, deeply moved again, came to the tomb; it was a cave, and a stone lay upon it. Jesus said, "Take away the stone." Martha, the sister of the dead man, said to him, "Lord, by this time there will be an odor, for he has been dead four days." Jesus said to her, "Did I not tell you that if you would believe you would see the glory of God?" So they took away the stone. And Jesus lifted up his eyes and said, "Father, I thank thee that thou hast heard me. I knew that thou hearest me always, but I have said this on account of the people standing by, that they may believe that thou didst send me." When he had said this, he cried with a loud voice, "Lazarus, come out." The dead man came out, his hands and feet bound with bandages, and his face wrapped with a cloth. Jesus said to them, "Unbind him, and let him go." Many of the Jews therefore, who had come with Mary and had seen what he did, believed in him.

Points to Ponder

Ezekiel 37:12-14

Ezekiel's message for the people of his time was that God can bring hope out of utter hopelessness. Because the truth of God is unchanging, that message is just as true for us as it was for the people of Judah.

This is the end of one of Ezekiel's most famous visions. The Spirit takes Ezekiel to a broad valley filled with bones.

And he said to me, "Son of man, can these bones live?"

And I answered, "O Lord GOD, you know."

Again he said to me, "Prophesy to these bones, and say to them, O dry bones, hear the word of the LORD. Thus says the Lord GOD to these bones: Behold, I will cause breath to enter you, and you shall live. And I will lay sinews upon you, and will cause flesh to come upon you, and cover you with skin, and put breath in you, and you shall live; and you shall know that I am the LORD."

So I prophesied as I was commanded; and as I prophesied, there was a noise, and behold, a rattling; and the bones came together, bone to its bone. And as I looked, there were sinews on them, and flesh had come upon them, and skin had covered them; but there was no breath in them.

Then he said to me, "Prophesy to the breath, prophesy, son of man, and say to the breath, Thus says the Lord GOD: Come from the four winds, O breath, and breathe upon these slain, that they may live."

So I prophesied as he commanded me, and the breath came into them, and they lived, and stood upon their feet, an exceedingly great host.

Then he said to me, "Son of man, these bones are the whole house of Israel. Behold, they say, 'Our bones are dried up, and our hope is lost; we are clean cut off.'"
—*Ezekiel 37:3-11*

This is where our reading picks up today. Like many prophecies in the Old Testament, this passage from Ezekiel has an immediate context and a more universal application.

The immediate context is the Babylonian Exile. The people of Judah had been utterly defeated: the Temple was destroyed, the people were in exile, and it seemed as if the exiles were nothing but dry bones. Ezekiel brings a message of hope: no matter how hopeless things seem to be, God is more powerful than our hopelessness. Dead bones can live again, and Israel can return from exile.

Many modern commentaries insist that this passage from Ezekiel has nothing to do with the resurrection of the dead: that it is *only* a metaphor for the redemption from captivity. But the Fathers of the Church are just about unanimous in seeing Ezekiel's vision as a prophecy of the resurrection.

> "And also through the prophet Ezekiel the resurrection of the dead was manifestly shown, when God brought him forth to the valley and showed him many bones, and made him pass by them round about them, and said to him, "Son of Man, can these bones live?" And Ezekiel said to him, "O Lord GOD, you know." —*Aphrahat, Demonstration 8, 12*

That is its more universal application. Prophecy often works that way. The passages from Isaiah that we read at Christmas predicted an heir to the throne of Israel in Isaiah's own time—but they also predicted the coming of the God the Son into the world. The history of Israel is itself a prophecy: as we heard on the first Sunday of Lent, Christians see "types" or images of things to come in the events of the Old Testament.

Romans 8:8-11

In Ezekiel's vision, the lifeless bodies come back to life when the *breath* enters them. "Breath," "wind," and "spirit" are the same word *ruah* in Hebrew and in Greek. For St. Paul, we are like those lifeless dry bones in Ezekiel unless the Spirit of God—the breath that entered the dead bodies of Israel—dwells in us.

Sin is what makes us dead. Because of sin we have no more hope than the dry bones in the valley. We live "in the flesh"—and that is the same as not really living at all. "To set the mind on the flesh is death," Paul said earlier (Romans 8:6), "but to set the mind on the Spirit is life and peace."

We know that God raised Jesus Christ from the dead and the same thing happens to us. We will be raised on the last day but notice that the way Paul sees it, we don't have to wait for the last day. We'll receive the completeness of all God's gifts then but already we have moved from death to life. When the Spirit entered us at baptism that Breath gave life to our lifeless mortality.

This is a good introduction to our Gospel reading today because we're about to hear the story a Lazarus, a close friend of Jesus who was raised from the dead. His resurrection is a sign of Christ's power over death, and—as St. Paul reminds us—that power is at work in us right now.

John 11:1-45

We've been introduced to this family in Luke's Gospel. Lazarus and his sisters Martha and Mary were close friends of Jesus. Luke tells us how Jesus visited the house of Mary and Martha, where Mary sat at his feet and listened while Martha worked in the kitchen (Luke 10:38-42). As our reading today tells us, it was Mary who would later anoint his feet with "costly ointment" and wipe them with her hair (John 12:3)—much offending Judas Iscariot, who thought the ointment could have been sold for a large sum, which he could then pocket himself (John 12:4-6).

Asking Jesus to come help was a big deal and the sisters would have known that. "The Jews" John's usual term for the Temple authorities who opposed Jesus had already decided that Jesus must die (John 5:18, 7:1). Jesus knew it was dangerous for him to set foot in Judea, and his disciples knew it as well.

They must have breathed twelve sighs of relief when Jesus said "This illness is not unto death," and made no move to head toward Judea. However, their relief turned to dismay when two days later he said, "Let us go into Judea again."

They must all be thinking the same thing: "We're all going to die." Thomas is the only one who puts that feeling into words: "Let us also go, that we may die with him."

They arrive in the middle of the mourning period, when many family friends are visiting to comfort Martha and Mary. Martha runs out to meet Jesus. She has the faith to say that Lazarus would not have died if Jesus had been there and she even has the faith to say that "whatever you ask from God, God will give you." When Jesus assures her that her brother will rise again, she answers, "I know that he will rise again in the resurrection at the last day."

All these things mark Martha as a woman of exemplary faith. Yet Jesus is about to demand even more faith from her when he says:

I am the resurrection and the life; he who believes in me, though he die, yet shall he live, and whoever lives and believes in me shall never die. Do you believe this?

What Jesus demands here is more than ordinary faith in God, in the resurrection of the dead and in himself as a prophet and healer sent by God. He demands that Martha believe that he *is* God.

Martha responds the way Christ wants us all to respond: "Yes, Lord; I believe that you are the Christ, the Son of God, he who is coming into the world."

When Mary sees Jesus, she repeats her sister's assertion that Lazarus would not have died if Jesus had been there and she dissolves into tears, Jesus is more deeply troubled than we have seen him so far in the entire Gospel story.

"Jesus wept", these are only two words in English and in Greek but one of the most profound statements in the whole of Scripture. God incarnate weeps for his creation: in that simple fact we have the reason for the Incarnation. God is immovable and perfect; but Jesus Christ was truly a man with a human being's joys and sorrows. He loved Lazarus, not just as God loves every created being but as a human being loves a good friend. He loves Mary and Martha too and their sorrow is heartbreaking to him.

St. Augustine reminded one of his correspondents who had lost her own brother that sorrow is natural, even when we know with absolute assurance that the ones we love will rise again.

"There is nothing in the sorrow of mortals over their dearly beloved dead that merits displeasure; but the sorrow of believers ought not to be prolonged. If, therefore, you have been grieved till now, let this grief be enough, and do not sorrow as the heathen, who "have no hope" (1 Thessalonians 4:12). For when the apostle Paul said this, he did not prohibit sorrow altogether, but only such sorrow as the heathen who have no hope show. For even Martha and Mary, pious sisters and believers, wept for their brother Lazarus, who they knew would rise again, though they did not know that he was to be restored to life at that time; and the Lord himself wept for that same Lazarus, whom he was going to bring back from death. Doubtless he permitted by his example here, though he did not by any precept demand, the shedding of tears over the graves even of those who we believe will rise again to the true life. "

—St. Augustine, Letter 263

Mary, as we know, was one of Jesus' most faithful followers. However, even she does not imagine that Jesus will be able to do anything for Lazarus now—not after he's been dead four days. The words "by this time there will be an odor" are translated very delicately for our modern tastes. The old Douay-Rheims version translated them "by this time he stinketh," and that is what Mary means: she expects an incredibly foul stench of rot if Jesus succeeds in having the stone rolled away. She has faith, but perhaps not *that* much faith. She believes in the resurrection but she doesn't believe she's going to see a preview of it right now.

Yet that is what happens. Lazarus walks out of the tomb—not a ghost of Lazarus, not an appearance of Lazarus' soul but Lazarus himself, still wrapped up in the grave clothes and doubtless stumbling awkwardly until Jesus reminds the gaping spectators that someone is going to have to unwrap the poor man.

This demonstration of Jesus' power over death causes many of the witnesses to believe in him and that is its main purpose in John's Gospel. John calls Jesus' miracles "signs"; they are physical demonstrations that Jesus is who we say he is. We see that purpose made explicit in Jesus' prayer: "Father, I thank you that you have heard me. I knew that you hear me always, but I have said this on account of the people standing by, that they may believe that you sent me."

Catechism Connections

- For a quick distinction between "flesh" and "spirit," see CCC 2819.
- To understand the Old Testament background of Christian belief in the resurrection, see CCC 992-996.
- For a deeper understanding of Jesus' prayer before the raising of Lazarus, see CCC 2604.
- For a brief explanation of Christian belief concerning the resurrection of the body, see CCC 997-1001.
- For what Christians believe about the resurrection "on the last day," see CCC 1038-1041.

Voices of the Saints

Among all the miracles wrought by our Lord Jesus Christ, the resurrection of Lazarus holds a foremost place in preaching. But if we consider attentively who did it, our duty is to rejoice rather than to wonder. A man was raised up by him who made man: for he is the only One of the Father, by whom, as you know, all things were made.

And if all things were made by him, what wonder is it that one was raised by him, when so many are daily brought into the world by his power? It is a greater deed to create men than to raise them again from the dead. Yet he deigned both to create and to raise again; to create all, to resuscitate some.

For though the Lord Jesus did many such acts, yet all of them are not recorded; just as this same St. John the evangelist himself testifies, that Christ the Lord both said and did many things that are not recorded; but such were chosen for record as seemed to suffice for the salvation of believers.

You have just heard that the Lord Jesus raised a dead man to life; and that is enough to let you know that, if he wished, he could raise *all* the dead to life. And, indeed this very work he has reserved in his own hands till the end of the world.

—*St. Augustine, Tractate 49 on the Gospel of John, 1*

Rome to Home

There are only two weeks to go until Easter and the Bible Readings of this Sunday all speak about resurrection. It is not yet that of Jesus, which bursts in as an absolute innovation, but our own resurrection, to which we aspire and which Christ himself gave to us, in rising from the dead. Indeed, death represents a wall as it were, which prevents us from seeing beyond it; yet our hearts reach out beyond this wall and even though we cannot understand what it conceals, we nevertheless think about it and imagine it, expressing with symbols our desire for eternity.

The Prophet Ezekiel proclaimed to the Jewish people, exiled far from the land of Israel, that God would open the graves of the dead and bring them home to rest in peace (cf. Ezekiel 37:12-14). This ancestral aspiration of man to be buried together with his forefathers is the longing for a "homeland" which welcomes us at the end of our earthly toil. This concept does not yet contain the idea of a personal resurrection from death, which only appears towards the end of the Old Testament, and even in Jesus' time was not accepted by all Judeans. Among Christians too, faith in the resurrection and in life is often accompanied by many doubts and much confusion because it also always concerns a reality which goes beyond the limits of our reason and requires an act of faith.

In today's Gospel — the raising of Lazarus — we listen to the voice of faith from the lips of Martha, Lazarus' sister. Jesus said to her: "Your brother will rise again," and she replies: "I know that he will rise again in the resurrection at the last day" (Jn 11:23-24). But Jesus repeats: "I am the resurrection and the life; he who believes in me, though he die, yet shall he live" (Jn 11:25-26). This is the true newness which abounds and exceeds every border! Christ pulls down the wall of death and in him dwells all the fullness of God, who is life, eternal life. Therefore death did not have power over him and the raising of Lazarus is a sign of his full dominion over physical death which, before God, resembles sleep (cf. Jn 11:11). However there is another death, which cost Christ the hardest struggle, even the price of the Cross: it is spiritual death and sin which threaten to ruin the existence of every human being. To overcome this death, Christ died and his Resurrection is not a return to past life, but an opening to a new reality, a "new land" united at last with God's Heaven. Therefore St Paul writes: "If the Spirit of him who raised Jesus from the dead dwells in you, he who raised Christ Jesus from will give life to your mortal bodies also through his Spirit who dwells in you" (Rom 8:11). Dear brothers and sisters, let us turn to the Virgin Mary, who previously shared in this Resurrection, so that she may help us to say faithfully: "Yes, Lord; I believe that you are the Christ, the Son of God" (Jn 11:27), to truly discover that he is our salvation.

—Benedict XVI Angelus, April 10, 2011

Study Questions

1. According to the word of the Lord to Ezekiel, what is the purpose of the resurrection of the dry bones? (See Points to Ponder)

2. How is Christ's power over death at work in us now? (See New Testament Reading)

3. According to this week's Gospel reading, why does Jesus delay when he hears that Lazarus is ill?

4. John makes as point of telling us that Jesus wept. Why did Jesus weep? (See John 11:4 and 11:25 to 11:33)

5. Why does John include the detail that Lazarus came out with "his hands and feet bound with bandages, and his face wrapped with a cloth"?

6. Why did Jesus raise Lazarus, knowing on the one hand that he would die again, and on the other that, as Mary said, he would be raised on the last day?

Lent Cycle A

Passion Sunday

Introduction

This is a Sunday of contrasts: we celebrate Christ's royal entry into Jerusalem and remember his suffering only a few days later.

When we read the passion narrative on this Sunday, the congregation often takes the part of the crowds clamoring for Christ's crucifixion. It's important for us to see how appropriate that is. Christ didn't die because people were much worse then than they are now. Christ died because we are all sinners and our sin is what crucifies him. Whenever we lapse into sin, we are that shouting crowd (see CCC 598). Yet Jesus Christ loves us well enough to sacrifice himself for us at the beginning of the first millennium and is still making that same sacrifice present on every altar in every parish church across the world.

Our Psalm today is Psalm 22, which begins, "My God, my God, why have you forsaken me?" When Jesus cries out those words from the cross, we may be tempted to hear them as a cry of despair. Though the Psalm describes in lively detail all the agonies Christ suffered it ends with triumphant confidence. Though we sing only excerpts from it today, we have enough to see the progression from suffering to assurance of God's mercy.

> All who see me mock at me,
>
> they make mouths at me, they wag their heads;
>
> "He committed his cause to the LORD; let him deliver him,
>
> let him rescue him, for he delights in him!"...
>
> Yea, dogs are round about me;
>
> a company of evildoers encircle me;
>
> they have pierced my hands and feet—
>
> I can count all my bones—
>
> they stare and gloat over me;
>
> they divide my garments among them,
>
> and for my raiment they cast lots.
>
> But you, O LORD, be not far off!
>
> O my help, hasten to my aid!...
>
> I will tell of your name to my brethren;
>
> in the midst of the congregation I will praise you:
>
> You who fear the LORD, praise him!
>
> all you sons of Jacob, glorify him,
>
> and stand in awe of him, all you sons of Israel!

Processional Reading: Matthew 21:1-11

And when they drew near to Jerusalem and came to Bethphage, to the Mount of Olives, then Jesus sent two disciples, saying to them, "Go into the village opposite you, and immediately you will find an ass tied, and a colt with her; untie them and bring them to me. If any one says anything to you, you shall say, 'The Lord has need of them,' and he will send them immediately." This took place to fulfil what was spoken by the prophet, saying, "Tell the daughter of Zion, Behold, your king is coming to you, humble, and mounted on an ass, and on a colt, the foal of an ass." The disciples went and did as Jesus had directed them; they brought the ass and the colt, and put their garments on them, and he sat thereon. Most of the crowd spread their garments on the road, and others cut branches from the trees and spread them on the road. And the crowds that went before him and that followed him shouted, "Hosanna to the Son of David! Blessed is he who comes in the name of the Lord! Hosanna in the highest!" And when he entered Jerusalem, all the city was stirred, saying, "Who is this?" And the crowds said, "This is the prophet Jesus from Nazareth of Galilee."

Old Testament Reading: Isaiah 50:4-7

The Lord GOD has given me the tongue of those who are taught, that I may know how to sustain with a word him that is weary. Morning by morning he wakens, he wakens my ear to hear as those who are taught. The Lord GOD has opened my ear, and I was not rebellious, I turned not backward I gave my back to the smiters, and my cheeks to those who pulled out the beard; I hid not my face from shame and spitting. For the Lord GOD helps me; therefore I have not been confounded; therefore I have set my face like a flint, and I know that I shall not be put to shame...

New Testament Reading: Philippians 2:6-11

Who, though he was in the form of God, did not count equality with God a thing to be grasped, but emptied himself, taking the form of a servant, being born in the likeness of men. And being found in human form he humbled himself and became obedient unto death, even death on a cross. Therefore God has highly exalted him and bestowed on him the name which is above every name, that at the name of Jesus every knee should bow, in heaven and on earth and under the earth, and every tongue confess that Jesus Christ is Lord, to the glory of God the Father.

Gospel Reading: Matthew 26:14-27:66

Due to the length of the Passion Reading, we ask that you refer to your Bible for the Gospel Reading.

Points to Ponder

The Gospel reading today is long and there is an extra Gospel reading for the procession with palms. The reading is densely packed with incident and meaning and it won't be possible to unpack all of it in one session.

What we'll try to do is understand a little of the context both historical and scriptural. We'll see how the passion of our Lord perfectly fulfills the prophecies of the Old Testament and we'll try to understand a little more of the historical conditions that made the trial and execution of Jesus take the course they took.

Matthew 21:1-11

Jesus' triumphal entry into Jerusalem is a completely improvised and unofficial thing—a spontaneous outpouring of enthusiasm from the crowds of ordinary citizens. We should take a moment to think how terrifying this triumph must have been both to the Roman occupiers and to the Jewish authorities who collaborated with them.

The Jewish authorities, hearing the crowds shouting "Hosanna to the son of David," would know that the words "son of David" can have only one meaning. The "son of David" is the legitimate heir to the throne of Israel, the *Messiah* or *anointed one*. Huge crowds of people in the capital of Judea are hailing this troublemaker Jesus, not just as a great prophet or teacher but also as the king of Israel. Palms are symbolic of victory—a procession with palms indicates a conquering hero. Jesus is entering Jerusalem not as an honored teacher or as a great prophet but as its victorious conqueror.

That presents an obvious problem for the Jewish authorities. The Roman Empire has always found Judea a troublesome province, full of religious fanatics who might erupt into riots at any moment and whose riots might easily flame up into full-scale rebellions. The Jewish authorities didn't like the Romans very much but it was necessary to get along with them well enough to keep business going. If they didn't put a stop to this potential revolution, the Romans might decide to do it themselves and the Romans might not be very careful in distinguishing who was a rebel and who was an innocent bystander.

This is an important part of the background for the Passion story. The triumphal entry into Jerusalem leads directly to the Passion. The Jewish authorities had long since decided that Jesus must die but the waving palms and shouting crowds made it obvious to them that it was dangerous to delay any longer.

They were about to get a lucky break. One of Jesus' inner circle would come to them and offer to hand him over. This is where our Gospel reading will begin.

Isaiah 50:4-7

This is one of the four chapters in Isaiah that Bible scholars call the Songs of the Suffering Servant.

Who is this servant? He is a representative of Israel but he is not identical to Israel. He brings the word of the Lord to the rest of Israel, "to sustain with a word him who is weary." In the end he will suffer alone for the sins of the people:

Surely he has borne our griefs and carried our sorrows; yet we esteemed him stricken, smitten by God, and afflicted. But he was wounded for our transgressions, he was bruised for our iniquities; upon him was the chastisement that made us whole, and with his stripes we are healed. All we like sheep have gone astray; we have turned every one to his own way; and the LORD has laid on him the iniquity of us all.
                                                                                                    —Isaiah 53:4-6

Christians have always seen the Suffering Servant as a prophetic image of Jesus Christ and in fact many Jewish writings have also interpreted them as prophecies of the coming Messiah.

We must include Jesus of Nazareth among those Jewish interpreters who saw Isaiah's Suffering Servant as a prophecy of the Messiah. We'll see in the main Gospel reading today how thoroughly Jesus matched the picture of the Suffering Servant in Isaiah. St. Paul also saw Jesus in the same context as we'll see in our next reading. This is important for us to understand because it's one of the chief arguments for Christianity throughout the ages.

The most effective argument of the early Christians, the one the first Christians writers made over and over, was how well Jesus fulfilled the prophecies in Scripture. It was not just an argument they made to Jewish believers—it was one they made over and over to pagans as well, converting them by thousands. When people saw how things that had been predicted centuries before were fulfilled in Jesus Christ, they believed, because the working of God in history was too obvious to ignore.

Philippians 2:6-11

When this reading follows the one from Isaiah, we can't help noticing how perfectly Christ fits the pattern of Isaiah's Suffering Servant.

The context of this reading is important. It describes Christ's whole earthly life as a pattern for us to follow:

So if there is any encouragement in Christ, any incentive of love, any participation in the Spirit, any affection and sympathy, complete my joy by being of the same mind, having the same love, being in full accord and of one mind. Do nothing from selfishness or conceit, but in humility count others better than yourselves. Let each of you look not only to his own interests, but also to the interests of others. Have this mind among yourselves, which is yours in Christ Jesus, who, though he was in the form of God...

—Philippians 2:1-5

Because we have Christ as our model, we should know how to be humble. It's human nature to think we're somehow special, better than other people. Christ really was better than other people and yet he "emptied himself."

What Paul emphasizes is how much Christ gave up for us: he was God but for our sake he became human, in such a way that no one who saw him without faith could see anything divine about him. He became the perfect Suffering Servant, obedient unto death. This very humility is the reason for our praise.

Many scholars see this passage as a very early Christian hymn quoted by St. Paul in his letter. It is very hymn-like in its praise of Christ's humility.

Matthew 26:14-27:66

Matthew's account of the Passion emphasizes, above all else, the fulfillment of the prophecies. This reading is a very long one even in the short form that some parishes may use.

Judas Betrays Jesus

The Gospel begins with one of the most baffling incidents in the whole New Testament: one of Jesus' own disciples sells his life to the Temple authorities.

Why did Judas betray Jesus? It's not an easy question to answer. The Gospel does not give us his inner thoughts: it only tells us what he did. According to Matthew, he made his decision right after the incident where a "woman", identified in The Gospel of John as Mary, the sister of Martha and Lazarus, anointed Jesus with costly ointment. Matthew reports that the disciples were "indignant" about the waste of money that could have been spent on the poor; John puts the indignation in the mouth of Judas the betrayer, adding, "This he said, not that he cared for the poor but because he was a thief, and as he had the money box he used to take what was put into it" (John 12:6).

Some interpreters have suggested that Judas was frustrated by Jesus' refusal to act like an earthly king. If Judas was greedy and ambitious, he might have been expecting to have a high position in the administration of the new king. Here, with the crowds waving palms and hailing Jesus as the Son of David, was the moment to seize power. Instead, Jesus was insisting that his kingdom was not an earthly kingdom at all. Where did that leave Judas?

On the other hand, it's possible that Judas was simply greedy for the money. Thirty pieces of silver was enough to buy a piece of land (Matthew 27:7) and the thief in Judas might not have been able to resist the temptation of so much money for so little work.

The Last Supper

Judas' betrayal comes just before the Passover meal that we know as the Last Supper—the central event of the week between Palm Sunday and Easter.

Matthew's account of the Last Supper is short. He gives us only the conversation about Judas' betrayal and the institution of the Eucharist.

The institution narrative in Matthew is very straightforward:

Now as they were eating, Jesus took bread, and blessed, and broke it, and gave it to the disciples and said, "Take, eat; this is my body." And he took a cup, and when he had given thanks he gave it to them, saying, "Drink of it, all of you; for this is my blood of the covenant, which is poured out for many for the forgiveness of sins. I tell you I shall not drink again of this fruit of the vine until that day when I drink it new with you in my Father's kingdom."

The thing that's missing here and in Mark's very similar version is the command, "Do this in remembrance of me." The narrative we usually hear in the liturgy is actually from one of St. Paul's letters, written (according to almost all Bible scholars) well before Matthew's Gospel:

For I received from the Lord what I also delivered to you, that the Lord Jesus on the night when he was betrayed took bread, and when he had given thanks, he broke it, and said, "This is my body which is for you. Do this in remembrance of me." In the same way also the cup, after supper, saying, "This cup is the new covenant in my blood. Do this, as often as you drink it, in remembrance of me." For as often as you eat this bread and drink the cup, you proclaim the Lord's death until he comes.

—1 Corinthians 11:23-26

It seems surprising that the conversation about betrayal gets as much prominence as the institution of the Eucharist, the central mystery of the Christian faith. The way the institution of the Eucharist follows the betrayal emphasizes the relationship. Judas' betrayal will lead to Jesus' death; at the Last Supper, Jesus is already offering his body and blood as a sacrifice. That would not happen without the betrayal of Judas.

We should not think that Judas was acting without free will. St. Leo the Great points out how many chances Jesus gave Judas to repent. Though he knew Judas would betray him, he did not keep him from sharing in the foundation of the Eucharist. When Jesus says that one of the twelve disciples will betray him, he doesn't name Judas, still giving him a chance to back down. Finally Judas himself asks, "Is it I, Master?" Jesus' response is "You have said so"—a way of speaking that indicates he wouldn't have said anything if Judas hadn't put him on the spot.

As he continues his sermon, St. Leo finds himself speaking directly to Judas, saying what every Christian would want to tell him: it's not too late. You can still repent.

But Jesus, sure of his purpose and undaunted in carrying out his Father's will, fulfilled the New Testament and founded a new Passover. For while the disciples were lying down with Him at the mystic Supper, and when discussion was proceeding in the hall of Caiaphas how Christ might be put to death, he, ordaining the Sacrament of his Body and Blood, was teaching them what kind of Victim must be offered up to God.

And not even from this mystery was the betrayer kept away, in order to show that he was exasperated by no personal wrong, but had determined beforehand of his own free will upon his treachery. For he was his own source of ruin and cause of perfidy, following the guidance of the devil and refusing to have Christ as director.

And so when the Lord said, "Truly, I say to you, one of you will betray me," he showed that his betrayer's conscience was well known to him—not confounding the traitor by harsh or open rebukes, but meeting him with mild and silent warnings, so that he who had never been sent astray by rejection might the easier be set right by repentance.

"Why, unhappy Judas, do you not make use of such great patience? Behold, the Lord spares your wicked attempts; Christ betrays you to none save yourself. Neither your name nor your person is discovered, but only the secrets of your heart are touched by the word of truth and mercy. The honor of the apostolic rank is not denied you, nor yet a share in the Sacraments. Return to your right mind; lay aside your madness and be wise. Mercy invites you, Salvation knocks at the door, Life recalls you to life. Look, your stainless and guiltless fellow disciples shudder at the hint of your crime, and all tremble for themselves till the author of the treachery is declared. For they are saddened not by the accusations of conscience, but by the uncertainty of man's changeableness; fearing lest what each knew against himself be less true than what the Truth Himself foresaw. "

"But you abuse the Lord's patience in this panic of the saints, and believe that your bold front hides you. You add impudence to guilt, and are not frightened by so clear a test. And when the others refrain from the food in which the Lord had set his judgment, you do not withdraw your hand from the dish, because your mind is not turned aside from the crime."
                                                        —*St. Leo the Great, Sermon 58, 3*

"The Son of man goes as it is written of him, but woe to that man by whom the Son of man is betrayed! It would have been better for that man if he had not been born."

Wasn't Judas' betrayal part of the divine plan and if that's the case, how can we blame Judas? St. John Chrysostom anticipated that question. It was part of the divine plan, he says, but Judas intended only evil. Although God brings good even out of the devil's schemes, that doesn't mean the devil is good.

"But someone will say, "Yet if it was written that he was to suffer these things, why do we blame Judas? For he did the things that were written."

But he did not do them with this intent, but from wickedness. For if you do not ask about the motive, you will deliver even the devil from the charges against him. But these things are not so, not at all. Both Judas and the devil are deserving of countless punishments, although the world was saved. It was not the treason of Judas that worked out salvation for us, but the wisdom of Christ, and the good contrivance of his fair skill, using the wickednesses of others for our advantage."
                                                        —*St. John Chrysostom, Homily 81 on Matthew, 2*

The Agony in the Garden

After the cup is passed, Jesus and his disciples go out to the Mount of Olives, just outside the city. There, Jesus tells the disciples that they will all run away and he also prophesies his own resurrection, promising to meet them in Galilee afterward. Peter insists that he will not fall away but Jesus foretells that he will deny his Master three times.

Gethsemane is on the slopes of the Mount of Olives; it's not called a "garden" here but it is in John (John 18:1). Here Jesus takes Peter, James, and John aside, the same three disciples who had seen his Transfiguration. They saw his divine glory then; now they will see his very human sorrow.

Jesus leaves them to wait while he prays, and his prayer is a cry of agony. Why does Christ pray to be spared the ordeal he knows is coming? Isn't he God? Doesn't he know how things will turn out?

Yes, but he is a man. His human nature was real. He had the human fear of pain and death: without them, he would not have been truly human.

St. John Chrysostom talks about Christ's humanity but he sees another reason. Christ's prayer in Gethsemane, he says, is a pattern for our own prayers. Whenever we are afraid, we should not be ashamed to pray to God to help us. We should also remember to end with "nevertheless, not as I will, but as you will."

When Christ had come to earth, he wished to instruct us in all virtue. Now the instructor teaches not only by word, but also by deed: for this is the teacher's best method of teaching.... Therefore the prayer which he wished to teach them, he himself also offered, speaking in a human way, not according to his Godhead (for the divine nature is impassable) but according to his humanity. And he prayed as instructing us to pray, and even to seek deliverance from distress; but, if this be not permitted, then to acquiesce in what seems good to God. Therefore he said "nevertheless, not as I will, but as you will": not because he had one will and the Father another; but in order that he might teach us even if we were in distress and trembling, even if danger came upon us, and we were unwilling to be torn from present life, nevertheless to postpone our own will to the will of God...
—*St. John Chrysostom, Homily on "Father, if it be possible..."*

Jesus Arrested

Jesus has just finished praying when a "great crowd with swords and clubs" shows up, with Judas at the front of it. Judas greets Jesus with a kiss, which is the sign for Jesus to be seized. One of the disciples—John says it was Peter (John 18:10)—has brought a sword and starts to fight to defend the Master. Jesus will not have violence. The scriptures must be fulfilled; once to his own disciples and once to the crowd that has come to haul him back to Jerusalem.

Jesus before Caiaphas

We see here how desperate the Temple authorities are to get rid of Jesus: "the chief priests and the whole council sought false testimony against Jesus that they might put him to death." Jesus himself refuses to answer any charges until the high priest Caiaphas puts him under oath, to which he answers again with a reluctant "You have said so."

With Jesus at last in their power, his enemies can't miss the opportunity for gratuitous cruelty. It is not enough to be rid of the troublemaker; they want revenge for all the times he got the better of them in an argument or seemed to be more popular than they were. But Jesus perfectly fulfills the words of Isaiah:

I was not rebellious, I turned not backward.

I gave my back to the smiters,

and my cheeks to those who pulled out the beard;

I hid not my face from shame and spitting.

Meanwhile, the disciples have all fled—fulfilling the prophecy, as Matthew, who was one of the cowards, points out. And they had good reason to be afraid. The crowd was looking for suspects. Three times someone is convinced that Peter, with his thick Galilean accent, must have been one of the followers of Jesus. Three times Peter feels the icy chill of terror and swears that he doesn't know Jesus. Only after the last denial does he remember what Jesus had said to him. "And he went out and wept bitterly."

Jesus before Pilate

The Temple authorities have jurisdiction in religious matters but the Romans do not allow them the power of capital punishment. Nothing but Jesus' death will make Caiaphas and his cronies feel safe. Thus they send Jesus to the Roman governor, Pontius Pilate, who is somewhat baffled by the whole proceeding.

Judas, meanwhile, has second thoughts but too late. Both Judas and Peter have betrayed Jesus. There is really only one difference: Peter weeps, but Judas despairs. Peter will go on and be forgiven; Judas does not believe that he can be forgiven. It was a terrible thing to betray the Master but it was also a terrible thing to deny the Master, as Peter did. The *unforgivable* sin of Judas is not the betrayal but his lack of faith in Christ's forgiveness. Matthew points out in Matthew: 27-9-10 how the tragic end of Judas fulfills the prophecies in Scripture. "Then was fulfilled what had been spoken by the prophet Jeremiah, saying, "And they took the thirty pieces of silver, the price of him on whom a price had been set by some of the sons of Israel, and they gave them for the potter's field, as the Lord directed me.""

Pilate is not at all interested in Jewish religion but the Temple authorities know how to play him. They make it look like there's about to be a riot, and riots are bad news. Judea is too prone to riots as it is and too much instability will lead to Pilate being recalled to Rome in disgrace. In fact, according to one tradition, that is exactly what eventually happened to Pilate in spite of all his efforts to keep things quiet.) Although he can find no reason to execute Jesus, he would rather sacrifice innocent blood than deal with another riot.

He gives the people one more chance to release Jesus but the Temple authorities have picked the right crowd and rehearsed them well. They demand Barabbas, a real criminal instead. (By a bitter irony, the name "Barabbas" means "son of the father" in Aramaic.)

So Jesus is condemned to die, and once again subjected to mockery and torture.

"What was done was the utmost limit of insolence. For not one member, but the whole entire body throughout was made an object of insolence; the head through the crown, and the reed, and the buffeting; the face, being spit upon; the cheeks, being struck with the palms of the hands; the whole body by the stripes, by being wrapped in the robe, and by the pretended worship; the hand by the reed, which they gave him to hold instead of a scepter; the mouth again by the offering of the vinegar. What could be more grievous than these things? What more insulting?..."

"And these things are read among us, when all meet together. So that the heathens may not say, "You show people and nations the things that are glorious and illustrious, such as the signs and the

miracles, but that you hide these which are matters of reproach," the grace of the Spirit has brought it to pass, that in the full festival, when men in multitude and women are present—and all, as one may say, at the great eve of the passover—then all these things should be read. When the whole world is present, then are all these acts proclaimed with a clear voice. And these being read, and made known to all, Christ is believed to be God and, besides all the rest, is worshiped, even because of this, that he deigned to stoop so much for us as actually to suffer these things, and to teach us all virtue."
—*St. John Chrysostom, Homily 87 on Matthew*

The Crucifixion

Crucifixion is not just a means of execution. It is designed to be agonizing and at the same time humiliating. The physical torture is unimaginable but the spiritual torture is at least as much of a horror. The victim was stripped naked and held up as a public display for people to mock. Usually it was a death reserved only for the worst possible offenders: people who were traitors against the Roman state.

At the point of death, Jesus cries out the first verse of Psalm 22. It sounds like a cry of despair but anyone who paid attention would have known that there was more to it than that. The first few words of a Psalm were like a title; by speaking them, Jesus was effectively quoting the whole Psalm, which moves from agony to triumphant confidence. Matthew, however, points out that many of the spectators couldn't hear Jesus clearly at all; they heard "Eli, Eli"—"My God, my God" and thought Jesus was calling for Elijah, whose name sounds very similar in Aramaic.

At the moment of Jesus' death, the curtain of the Temple was torn in two. The curtain separated the Holy of Holies, where God dwelt on earth, from the rest of the Temple. With Jesus' death on the cross, there is no more separation between God and sinners. The veil that keeps us away from God's presence is torn away.

The Burial of Jesus

A very brave man, Joseph of Arimathea, came to Pilate and asked for the body of Jesus. Normally the bodies of crucified criminals were thrown out for the beasts to devour but Pilate may have been feeling some guilt over having condemned an innocent man. The Temple authorities were worried that someone would steal the body and Matthew takes care to point out that they persuaded Pilate to seal the tomb and post a guard there.

They placed Jesus in the tomb and his followers kept a very somber Sabbath. They must have wondered whether everything they had done, everything they had believed and hoped for, was all for nothing.

They were about to get the surprise of their lives.

Lenten Moment

In the town of Saint-Gilles in France is a magnificent Romanesque abbey church, long considered one of the masterpieces of medieval architecture. Above the entrance portico is a long frieze depicting in relief the events of Holy Week, beginning with Palm Sunday and ending with the Crucifixion.

Right in the middle, above the main door, is the Last Supper.

The symbolism is wonderfully appropriate. The Last Supper is the spiritual center of Holy Week. As you walk through that door into the church you enter the Last Supper. You go in to participate in the sacrament Christ instituted at that meal, the sacrament that is still going on in every Catholic Church across the world. The architecture and sculpture work so well together that, when Andrew Carnegie surveyed the top American architects of his era, to ask which monuments should be represented in his new museum, this church was at the top of every single list. Carnegie had a full-size cast made of the entire entrance portico, and it's still in his museum in Pittsburgh today in the gigantic Hall of Architecture, as the star exhibit in a gallery of the architectural masterpieces of the world.

Holy Week begins with Palm Sunday and ends with Holy Saturday. It begins with Christ triumphant and ends with Christ dead and buried. Next week, of course, begins with the joyful celebration of Easter but this week is our time to meditate on the events that worked out our salvation.

The centerpiece is the Eucharist. Christ's death on the cross, defeated death and sin but it is the Eucharist that makes Christ's saving sacrifice present to us all in all our churches. Every time we walk through the door to go to Mass, we walk right into that meal in which Christ offered his body and blood to his disciples.

Catechism Connections

- To understand better what it meant for the Son of God to "empty himself," see CCC 472.

- To see how the institution of the Eucharist fulfilled the Passover, see CCC 1337-1340.

- To understand how the Last Supper is related to our celebration at Mass today, see CCC 1341-1344.

- For the meaning of the agony at Gethsemane, see CCC 612.

- For a useful reminder of the "historical complexity" of Jesus' trial, see CCC 597.

- To see how we are called to participate in Christ's sacrifice on the cross, see CCC 618.

Voices of the Saints

Whenever anything disagreeable or displeasing happens to you, remember Christ crucified and be silent.

—St. John of the Cross

Rome to Home

As the Lenten journey, which began with Ash Wednesday, nears its end, today's liturgy for Wednesday of Holy Week already introduces us into the dramatic atmosphere of the coming days, steeped in the memory of the Passion and death of Christ. In fact, in today's liturgy, the Evangelist Matthew presents for our meditation the brief dialogue between Jesus and Judas that took place in the Upper Room.

"Is it I, Master?" the traitor asked the divine Teacher, who had foretold: "Truly, I say to you, one of you will betray me." The Lord's answer was incisive: "You have said so" (cf. Mt 26: 14-25). For his part, John concludes the narrative announcing Judas' betrayal with a few portentous words: "It was night" (Jn 13: 30). When the traitor left the Upper Room, thick darkness gathered in his heart—it was an inner night— bewilderment increased in the hearts of the other disciples—they too were moving towards night— while the steadily darkening twilight of abandonment and hatred hung over the Son of Man who was preparing to consummate his sacrifice on the Cross. What we shall be commemorating in the coming days is the supreme battle between Light and Darkness, between Life and Death. We must also put ourselves in this context aware of our own "night," of our sins and our responsibility, if we want to benefit spiritually from the Paschal Mystery, if we want our hearts to be enlightened through this Mystery which constitutes the central fulcrum of our faith.

—Benedict XVI, General Audience, April 4, 2007

Study Questions

1. In the Gospel of Matthew reading we are told that Jesus rode into Jerusalem on a colt of an ass. This was prophesized by the prophet Zechariah (See Zech. 9:9-10). What is the significance of Jesus riding on a donkey? (See 1st Kings 1:33; Judges 5:10, 10:4, 12:14 and 2nd Samuel 16:2.

2. Why is the Last Supper the center of Holy Week? (See Exodus 11:1-13:16 and CCC1324)

3. According to Church teaching, how does Jesus' celebration of the Last Supper with the disciples in the course of a Passover meal give meaning to the Jewish Passover (see *CCC* 1340)?

4. How is the sacrament of the Eucharist tied to forgiveness of sins? How does Jesus' sacrifice echo the sacrifice involved in the Old Covenant entered into with God by Moses on behalf of the 12 tribes of Israel (see *Ex* 24:8)?

5. Why did Jesus pray at Gethsemane to be spared from the agony to come? (see Hebrews 4:15)

6. How is Jesus' prayer at Gethsemane a model for our own prayers? (See Points to Ponder)

7. Why couldn't Judas be forgiven, though Peter could? (See Points to Ponder and last week's New Testament reading from Romans 8:8-11)

Suggested
Responses

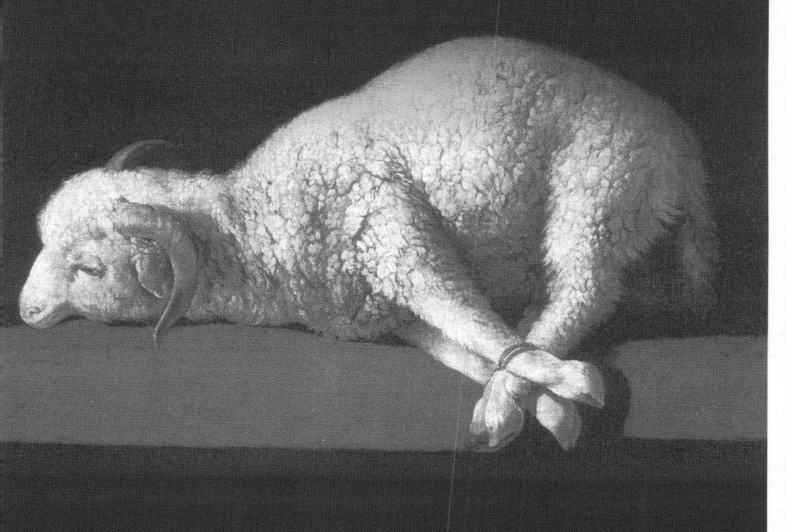

Lent Cycle A

Suggested Responses

Week 1:

1. Genesis 2:7 states: "then the LORD God formed the man* out of the dust of the ground and blew into his nostrils the breath of life, and the man became a living being".

2. Genesis 3:7 states that as soon as they sinned and ate the fruit they felt ashamed. "Then the eyes of both of them were opened, and they knew that they were naked; so they sewed fig leaves together and made loincloths for themselves." Gn 3:7

3. According to St Paul, Adam "was a type of the one who was to come." St. Paul tells us in Romans that as one man's (Adam's) disobedience many were made sinners and by one man's (Christ's) obedience many will be made righteous. For as by one man's disobedience many were made sinners, so by one man's obedience many will be made righteous.

4. Man could do nothing to deserve justification. It didn't happen because we were very good and finally deserved life instead of death. We are justified because God chooses to give us freely, out of his own overflowing love, the gift of redemption by sending his Son to undo that damage.

5. The devil used Christ's human hunger as a temptation, telling him "If you are the Son of God, command that these stones become loaves of bread." Christ's resistance to the devil's temptation, "It is written, 'Man shall not live by bread alone, but by every word that proceeds from the mouth of God.'" is the exact opposite response of Adam and Eve who ate of the fruit they were forbidden to eat.

6. Satan tempts Christ to prove he is the Son of God and encourages him to throw himself from the top of the temple, taunting that if he is the Son, God will send his angels to protect him. Jesus said to him, "Again it is written, 'You shall not tempt the Lord your God.'"

7. In Matthew's Gospel we read that again Satan tempted Christ a third time by offering him all the kingdoms of the world if he would fall down and worship Satan. Then Jesus said to him, "Begone, Satan! for it is written, 'You shall worship the Lord your God and him only shall you serve.'"Suggested Responses

Week 2

1. Abram has very little knowledge of where God is telling him to go. The only information he has is, "To the land that I will show you".

2. The calling of Abraham, the calling of Jesus' disciples and the calling of ordinary Christians are similar. In all cases, they are being called on a journey whose end can't be seen but by faith they know that God will keep his promises. The disciples were just told, "Follow me," and Christ makes the same demand of us today.

3. Although Jesus of Nazareth was born at a particular time in history that was still within living memory when Paul wrote, the Son of God existed from the beginning, and the plan of salvation was set from the moment of creation. The Gospel of John begins: "In the beginning was the Word" (John 1:1).

4. Peter reacts by suggesting that they build three tents, one for each of the glorious figures. In the Gospel of Mark we learn that Peter didn't know what to say, which suggests that he was completely overwhelmed. [In class discussions, it may be useful to point out what a human reaction this is: the Transfiguration was a supernatural event, but it was witnessed by real people who reacted the way any human being would react to something awe-inspiring and inexplicable.]

5. According to St. Leo, Moses and Elijah represent the whole of the Old Testament, known as "the Law and the Prophets" in Jewish tradition. Thus we see the Old Testament Scriptures, the only ones known to Jesus' disciples, witnessing to the divinity of Christ.

6. Some parallels between the Transfiguration and Moses' encounter with God in the Old Testament include: high mountain, shining face and voice from a cloud.

Week 3

1. Moses asks God to provide water for the Isrealites and their cattle so they will not die. God tells Moses, "Behold, I will stand before you there on the rock at Horeb; and you shall strike the rock, and water shall come out of it, that the people may drink." Horeb, which is another name for Sinai and the specific place was called Massah and Meribah.

2. According to St Paul's Letter to the Romans we have reason to hope because God's love has been poured into our hearts through the Holy Spirit which has been given to us.

3. Jesus asked the Samaritan woman at the well to give him a drink. "The Samaritan woman said to him, "How is it that you, a Jew, ask a drink of me, a woman of Samaria?" For Jews have no dealings with Samaritans. Jesus answered her, "If you knew the gift of God, and who it is that is saying to you, 'Give me a drink,' you would have asked him, and he would have given you living water."

4. Jesus reveals that he is the Messiah, The woman said to him, "I know that Messiah is coming (he who is called Christ); when he comes, he will show us all things." Jesus said to her, "I who speak to you am he." The fact that Jesus revealed who he was for the first time in John's Gospel to a Samaritan woman is quite extraordinary because Jews did not have dealings with Samaritans, let alone a woman and especially a woman who was living outside of wedlock and had several husbands.

5. Christ's disciples were amazed that he was speaking with the Samaritan woman but said nothing, "but still no one said, "What are you looking for?" or "Why are you talking with her?"

6. At first, many Samaritans believe because of the woman's testimony. Many more believed because Jesus stayed with them for two days and they believed because of his word. "They said to the woman, "It is no longer because of your words that we believe, for we have heard for ourselves, and we know that this is indeed the Savior of the world.

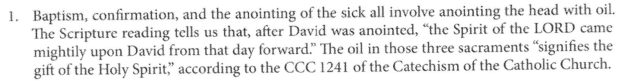

Week 4

1. Baptism, confirmation, and the anointing of the sick all involve anointing the head with oil. The Scripture reading tells us that, after David was anointed, "the Spirit of the LORD came mightily upon David from that day forward." The oil in those three sacraments "signifies the gift of the Holy Spirit," according to the CCC 1241 of the Catechism of the Catholic Church.

2. When St. Paul tells us to "expose" the "works of darkness," it's tempting for us to point fingers at people we consider sinners. But perhaps the exposure starts with exposing the works of darkness in ourselves. When Jesus said that we should not judge unless we be judged also, he was not saying that we are never to judge if behavior is sin or not. He was was cautioning us to make sure that we are willing to be judged by the same standard of judgment. The verse in Matthew 7:1 is not a warning against judging an action but rather a warning against self-deception and hypocrisy. We have to look at the context of the statement. The following verse helps explain what Jesus is saying: "For in the way you judge, you will be judged and by your standard of measure, it will be measured to you." (Matthew 7:2) In other words, if you are going to say that what someone else is doing is wrong then you should be prepared to be judged by the same standard.

3. Drinking to excess is often either a search for euphoria or an attempt to escape misery. St. Paul seems to suggest that the Christian life, lived to the fullest, is real euphoria far superior to the artificial euphoria produced by alcohol and overindulgence. It is also the only sure way out of the misery brought on us by sin.

4. The divine power of Christ shows itself in healing the blind man. The healing also shows how wrong it is to assume that blindness is a punishment for sin: God didn't make the world that way. There is room here for an open-ended discussion of how your parish helps people with various disabilities, but one way of keeping the discussion on track is to keep bringing it back to making the works of God manifest. What do people see when they look at our parish? Do they see a comfortable suburban social club, or do they see a place where the works of God are done daily by the hands of his people?

5. Outward washing is a sign of spiritual cleansing. The sacraments were foreshadowed in the OT by things that didn't actually convey grace but were mere symbols (for example, circumcision prefigured baptism; the Passover meal prefigured the Eucharist.) When Christ came he made them more than symbols. During his earthly ministry Jesus healed, fed and strengthened people through humble elements such as mud, water, bread, oil and wine. He could have performed his miracles directly but he preferred to use material things to bestow his grace. There is always a material element in a sacrament. Grace builds on nature; God chooses to confer his grace through the material world he created.

6. Although the individuals' sins did not produce the blindness, all suffering in this world is ultimately the result of sin but it's because of original sin, the sin of our first parents Adam and Eve, which comes down to us as their descendants.

Lesson 5

1. God directs Ezekiel to tell the people in exile, "You shall know that I am the Lord" They might doubt God but when God brings them back to Israel they will know that God has been there all the time.

2. St. Paul says, "if Christ is in you, although your bodies are dead because of sin, your spirits are alive because of righteousness." Sin—according to St. Paul—makes us no better than dead bodies. But the Holy Spirit entered us at baptism, and we are given the grace to overcome sin.

3. The text suggests that Jesus knew Lazarus would die and that it was necessary for the belief of his followers that they should see Lazarus raised from the dead. Judea was a very dangerous place for Jesus and there is an opportunity for an open-ended discussion of how Jesus' humanity affects his mission—a discussion that can certainly continue next week in the passion narrative.

4. John is emphasizing that Jesus experienced a full range of human emotions. and was "deeply moved in spirit, "troubled" and "wept". Jesus was "deeply moved in spirit, "troubled" and "wept" when he saw his friend Mary weeping (John 11:33). He feels overwhelming compassion for his friends in their mourning; their grief over Lazarus' death represents all the sorrow of all the generations since Adam.

5. The Gospel of John includes details concerning Lazarus' appearance because it demonstrates that Lazarus was really dead: his family had spent some time with the body carefully preparing it for the tomb.

6. Jesus' response to Mary is "I am the resurrection and the life," and the resurrection of Lazarus demonstrates that Jesus speaks the truth. Seeing Lazarus walking out of the tomb, many people believed in Jesus: they had irrefutable proof that he had power over death. It seems that what Jesus did was not for the sake of Lazarus but for the sake of all.

Week 6

1. In the ancient Middle Eastern world, leaders rode horses if they rode to war, but donkeys if they came in peace. We see in 1st Kings that Solomon rode a donkey on the day he was recognized as the new king of Israel. In Zechariah the description of a king is one who is righteous and gentle. Rather than riding to conquer, this king entered in peace. Unfortunately those who welcomed him with palm branches and shouts of Hosanna (which means "Save us") chose to ignore that he was coming in peace and offering them spiritual freedom. They instead chose to see him as a warrior king who would free them from Roman authority. This is why the same crowd turned on him a week later, crying "Crucify him" because he didn't fulfill their "worldly" needs and expectations.

2. The Passover feast was an especially holy event for the Jewish people in that it remembered the time when God spared them from the plague of physical death in Egypt through the shedding of the blood of a spotless lamb. The lamb in the Old Testament prefigures Christ, who is sinless (spotless) and the true sacrificial Lamb of God who sheds his blood on the cross to save us from our sins. Jesus chose the Passover supper as the time to introduce a new covenant and institute the Eucharist which is the Sacrament by which his sacrifice on the cross is made present to us at every Mass. At the last supper with his apostles, Jesus nourished them with his body and blood just as he does for us still. His body is true food and his blood is true drink (John 6:55) The Eucharist is the source and summit of our faith "for in the blessed Eucharist is contained the whole spiritual good of the Church" (CCC 1324)

3. Paragraph 1340 of the *Catechism of the Catholic Church* teaches: "By celebrating the Last Supper with his apostles in the course of the Passover meal, Jesus gave the Jewish Passover its definitive meaning. Jesus' passing over to his Father by his death and Resurrection, the new Passover, is anticipated in the Supper and celebrated in the Eucharist, which fulfills the Jewish Passover and anticipates the final Passover of the Church in the glory of the kingdom."

4. In Matthew 26:28, Jesus uses words that make it clear the sacrament is irrevocably tied to the forgiveness of sins: "[F]or this is my blood of the covenant, which is poured out for many for the forgiveness of sins." Forgiveness will be accomplished by Jesus' death, which is the sacrifice that seals the covenant bond between God and his people. This echoes the covenant sacrifice described in Exodus 24:8: "And Moses took the blood and threw it upon the people, and said, 'Behold the blood of the covenant which the LORD has made with you in accordance with all these words.'"

5. In Hebrews 4:15 St. Paul states, "For we have not a high priest who is unable to sympathize with our weaknesses, but one who in every respect has been tempted as we are, yet without sin." Jesus was both fully human and fully divine, meaning that he not only knew what he was about to suffer but in his human nature he felt anguish and dread concerning what he was to endure. Some Christians believed that Jesus was a divine being who only put on the appearance of a man but in reality did not suffer at all when he was crucified. To believe this is heresy. Jesus took on our sins and suffered horrific agony on the cross for our sake.

6. Some Christians erroneously believe that it is selfish for one to pray to be relieved of their trials or suffering. While it is true that we should offer up our sufferings for others, it is not wrong or selfish to pray to be spared or for relief. As St. John Chrysostom suggests, we should imitate Jesus in praying to be spared from trials but at the same time we should always pray,

just as Jesus did, that not our will, but God's will be done. As Christians, we should always put God's Will ahead of our own. Even though we may not understand why we must suffer some things, we need to trust that God loves us and His will is best so perhaps the best prayer during trials would be to not only offer up our sufferings but to ask for God's grace to help us endure them.

7. Instead of seeking forgiveness, Judas despaired and hung himself. The sin against the Holy Spirit, the one that cannot be forgiven, is the sin of final impenitence. God can forgive any repented sin, but man must repent of his sins before he can be forgiven. As only God can judge hearts, we cannot know whether Judas was impenitent to his very death, but we can know that he did not demonstrate the heroic virtue of Peter, who repented his betrayal of Christ rather than allow despair to consume him. While Judas did feel remorse for what he did (Mt 27:3-4), he chose the wrong means to demonstrate that remorse (Mt 27:5) and he may have had the selfish reasons for his remorse as well. St. Paul said that "those who are in the flesh cannot please God." We know that Judas was "in the flesh – living according to the ways of the world, rather than being in the Spirit because 1) He made a conscience choice to betray Jesus - Luke 22:48; 2) He was a thief with greed in his heart - John 12:6.; 3) Jesus knew Judas' heart was set on evil and that he would not repent - John 6:70, John 17:12.

Printed in the United States
By Bookmasters